You
By D.K.

Copyright © D.K

This edition published in 2019

The right of D.K. Daniels to be identified as the author of this work has been asserted by him in accordance with the Copyright, Designs and Patents Act 1988 and the Irish Copyright and Related Rights Act 2000.

Because of the dynamic nature of the Internet, any web addresses or links contained in this book may have changed since publication and may no longer be valid. The views expressed in this work are solely those of the author for the purpose of the story.

Any people depicted in stock imagery provided by Adobe Stock, are models and such images are being used for illustrative purposes only.

Adobe Stock Images ©

All rights reserved. No part of this publication may be reproduced, transmitted, or stored in a retrieval system, in any form or by any means, without permission in writing from the publisher, nor be otherwise circulated in any form of binding or cover other than that in which is is published and without a similar condition being imposed on the subsequent purchaser.

All characters in this publication are fictitious and any resemblance to real people, alive or dead, is purely coincidental.
For more information on books, updates and all that fun-stuff visit my website.
www.dk-daniels.com

Cover Design

By Shommy
For business enquiries contact Shommy through 99designs.
https://99designs.ie/profiles/shommy

CONTENTS

Acknowledgments	v
Entry #1	1
Entry #2	3
Entry #3	5
Entry #4	8
Entry #5	12
Entry #6	16
Entry #7	22
Entry #8	29
Entry #9	36
Entry #10	45
Entry #11	53
Entry #12	61
Entry #13	69
Entry #14	81
Entry #15	94
Entry #16	112
Entry #17	137
Entry #18	169
Entry #19	186
Entry #20	191
Entry #21	195
Entry #22	199
Entry #23	204
Entry #24	210
Entry #25	215
Entry #26	219
Entry #27	224
Entry #28	230
Entry #29	239

Also by D.K. Daniels	249
Afterword	251
About the Author	253

ACKNOWLEDGMENTS

For my mother, who taught me to love the power of my imagination and creativity.

To my father for giving me the love of entertaining.

And for my loving boyfriend who has been exceptionally forbearing when my emotions change like the Irish weather.

I'd like to extend a thank you to Larry Osburn who provided countless hours to ensure the original book meets a quality level. Time being the most valuable commodity, I am eternally grateful for his patience and diligence. Any errors remaining are of my own doing.

YOU & I

D.K. DANIELS

To Anna

I hope you enjoy my book,
Thanks

David Mooney - Aka D.K. Daniels

23/11/2019

ENTRY #1

Hi, I guess.

I'M NOT TOO sure what to write here other than hi... It's weird you know because I have been assigned a pen-pal, which is obviously outdated dude or girl or whatever. I'm a dude, well, I'm fourteen, and since I have no idea who the anonymous person I have been forced to write to for the next two months, I don't know what to say.

For the next couple of weeks, are we supposed to be super simple and not get much into things in order to pass the class. I'm not going to lie I need to make an effort, my grades are super-bad, so if you make an effort, I'll make an effort. I'll confess it is a little weird to talk to another person without saying my name. I've been told it has to be secret, and that seems odd, due to the fact the first thing I have been conditioned to do is state my name the first time I meet someone new.

Our teacher told us today we are supposed to write our notes and place them in the box at the front of the classroom to distribute the letters to and from you. So, to state for the record, and from what number I picked on the form, I choose candidate 37, which is you whoever you are. I don't feel like calling you candidate 37. Despite, it seems impersonal, and I don't know it seems wrong to call another human by a number, but whatever. Perhaps call me Bond... James Bond.

I WROTE the letter you're reading three times. I am sorry if it is cringy and you are already dreading the coming days and contact with me. I ran out of time to write anything because I had to start over so many times. I get nervous sometimes; I don't know why I guess it is in my nature. At least I have the comfort in knowing the teachers won't read what we are writing, and it is going to be funny building a conversation with someone I have probably, or probably have not met. The chance and probability, however, are quite high considering we are in the same school. The forwarding number states this school.

ANYWAY, it's almost home time, and I have basketball practice to do so; I hope you have a nice day.

FROM,
    Bond... James Bond.

ENTRY #2

To Mr. James Bond,

Ello, to you too. Your snarkasm is duly noted, and I find it amusing, plus don't be afraid, I believe I am as nervous about writing what I am writing as of this moment as you were when you were sending me the letter. I am a boy too, 14 also, at least I got another guy to talk to. I don't talk to many guys because not to many take notice.

Personally, I presume I would have fallen out of my chair if I received a girl. I have been wondering all day who I have been assigned to and I know I can't say any kind of thank you for picking me because chances are you have no idea who I am.

I agree a number is impersonal and I am glad you have chosen to point it out in our first letter. I guess it would be hard to communicate calling each other Candidate(A) and Candidate(B.)

. . .

Anyhow, I'll help you out, no problem, I'm not bad off when it comes to grades so I guess I can relax a little, but not too much. My parents would kill me if I fail any exams and I don't want to live through it. I'll write to you as long as you write to me, plus I guess it indicates the two of us have to keep on lettering if we want to advance. I'll get by, but extra credits are always welcome. The letter was fine; personally, I did not find it awkward so you can cool it.

From what I can tell, and with the tone of your voice coming through in the letter, you seem like a nice person, who wants to be honest. I try to be frank except it doesn't help me all the same.

It sounds like you are famous or something, well you must be if you are on the basketball team. I would never sign up for it. I can't imagine myself being flung around the court like some dogs waterlogged stick. I am a little skinny, so I suppose I am not one for sports. Combine it with the fact I have no interest in the concept, then it makes sense. I belong elsewhere, commonly where folks don't see me or where I can't hear them.

I have a mountain of homework to do when I get home. Send help.

Until next time,
    Sherlock

ENTRY #3

To Sherlock,

Does that imply you are a detective? Figuring you chose to be called Sherlock? I recently completed binge-watching season four of the TV show on Netflix, I assume it was on Monday. It is probably the reason I got in trouble, or it was the last straw anyhow. I dozed off and got into shit in class the following morning for not finishing my English essay. Therefore, thank you very much, Sherlock... Do you possess a Watson, can I be the guy who tags along because you sound intelligent, so perhaps Sherlock is a fitting nickname? Watson is the dumb dude who pretends to be smart rather than doing anything helpful. Right?

My Basketball practice was okay, I guess. I was zonked by the time I finished up, and when I got home, a shower never felt so good. My position on the team is a shooting guard.

I'm not sure if I am supposed to share this sort of information because I'm not sure if it gives away my identity although anyway it's out there now. In a couple of weeks, we have a game coming up, and I don't believe I am ready for it. I have been crappy the last couple of sessions, plus my shots have been off, I don't know why though.

About being truthful, I guess I would use the word honest. I know that if someone were leading me on, I would not like it. Therefore, I prefer not to go down that path. I'm kind of a, "what you see is what you get guy." I take everything in stride, and I hope somewhere along the line I haven't offended someone.

LMFAO, ...dogs waterlogged stick. I've never heard the expression before. I haven't smiled all day so if you want to know you made a miserable hour seem a little lighter. How do you know you wouldn't enjoy sports if you are not willing to try it? From the sounds of it, you haven't attempted. Plus, what do you mean you would rather be away in a corner where people don't notice you. I don't think what you said is positive about yourself; you need to be optimistic. I suppose be prepared to try. I remember the first time I tried out in band practice. I felt so out of place, I knew nobody, although most recognized me. I gained some sweet new friends due to it, so it's better than not attempting to work at it.

OH, and message received, help returned. I give you the almighty power of Kratos from God Of War to help you shift the mountain of homework.

. . .

From,
> Bond... James Bond.

ENTRY #4

To Mr. James Bond,

Yes, please do, send the power of the gods I require it. I spent all last night having to do algebra. By the point, I had concluded my assignments, my mind was spinning with all the problems that were required to be solved. Actually, my head is still paining me today at the amount of pages our math teacher lumbered us with. Do educators never take into account how much homework we get from several other teachers? They say they are busy correcting our exams on an occasional basis when they are at home on the weekends. Don't they have a life outside the classroom? Furthermore, when we don't have our coursework done in the off chance, they get all up-tight.

The "*I don't have my paper corrected*" doesn't work, and the worst part of it all is, seldom it is not intended. I have half a mind to say well if you were so goddam busy during the weekend, as not to return my exams papers on Monday.

The one I completed on Friday, then don't expect me to have the assignment you gave me on Friday, to be finished for Monday. Bag that and ship it to all your other teacher friends.

The irony in the teachers' speech, "*I had other students schoolwork to correct,*" is getting old, don't you say. I wish I could walk up to the occasional mentor and say, "I *have other teachers homework to do.*" Ah... I'm indulging myself, as it would ever happen or I'd have the balls to pull off such an act.

And, no I have no Watson, I suppose I am at a loss as to having a partner in crime as so to speak. I don't think I would make a very good partner in crime. I am not cut out for all the running and climbing you see in the detective shows. I am content with a big bag of Cheetos and a TV, instead of all that physical exercise.

Plus, Sherlock may be the brains for the operation, but Watson is the dude who keeps track of everything, so you have to thank yourself for being a formidable secretary. I decided Sherlock because I spend a great deal of my time in reflection, reading books and well I guess I am a little geeky but not too much. I don't fit the iconic 1980s nerds or anything, so let's hope to say you don't meet the stereotypical jock trope from the 1980s.

SORRY TO HEAR you are not as productive as you'd hoped. I wish it picks up for you and soon. I would come to one of the Basketball games if I knew who I was rooting for, but this is the beauty of being secretive here. Perhaps you'll never know. I might turn up, even though I have no inkling who you are or what you look like. I reckon if I did go, I'd have to be on the lookout for a guy who likes Basketball, who has a habit of not doing his school work and most certainly looks like a Watson. Okay, I got it, I've secured it in my mind palace for future analysis.

I do try to do sports, except it's not for me. I end up being more of a hassle for the team and the people in the group. Plus, there is a whole other fuss which makes me stupid on any court, field, or track. I occasionally try to do some swimming as it can be done in my own time and people don't get all up in your business about it. I like it when I shift through the water; it is soothing and relaxing. I can't quite explain it.

Good to know I made you smile, it's comforting to know I made you grin at least. I used to do band, but I dropped out, I wasn't excellent. I used to play Clarinet, and the teacher said I was great, but all around me, I knew people were talking about me and my crappy ability.

So, as I bring this letter to a close; I have a couple of questions.

1.) What instrument do you play in the band?

2.) And are you a movie or game enthusiast because you seem to have an interest? You mentioned a game the last time.

Anyway, I hope your next Basketball practice goes well. Please write back to me when you can.

. . .

Ps, what you say to being called Watson?

From,
    Sherlock

ENTRY #5

To Sherlock,

I HAVE TRANSFERRED the power of Kratos via FedEx; you should receive it within 2-3 working days. I presume here is where the two of us will beg to differ. I would not in all of my days lose sleep over something as stupid as homework. Sleep is much too valuable to lose rest to something extremely petty. Teachers would not suffer sleep for you, therefore why should you for them. If I do homework, which is even a hassle to get me to sit down, it will solely be in a quick burst of twenty minutes to forty. After that, I could not care less about the work getting done. I don't understand why they think it is appropriate to grade and observe us like a bunch of rats in a maze or a specimen in a petri dish. I believe we have passed that test, then why don't they show us they also have.

On the contrary, Math is one of my strong points. Still, I don't know why I don't invest any more time in perfecting it. Just wait and see; next, the government will have weird kids who can do weird stuff with their minds like from some sad sci-fi flick, they'll be bending spoons alone with brain waves.

AMEN, I will accept that, preach! Teachers have no idea how much shit they dish out. I'm not sure if you prefer not to cuss, but in the likelihood, I am sorry. I would have no problem saying something as you've outlined in the letter. Except, I would rather not because I am in hot water. Therefore, I have to be "*GOOD*" as the adults say. I'll hold you to the gesture although, once I get out of this mess I've gotten myself into I'll tell a teacher what you said.

I am not afraid of teachers, well perhaps Mr. Murphy, he always looks stern, as if he is ready to leap up over a desk like a Demogorgon and have at you. I can imagine it. He'll leach his face to mine; the teeth will pop right into the velvet of my skin as if he were eating an apricot. Which ironically, he does eat every Biology class; amusingly it is fitting. The blooded ooze, flowing the decent of my checks held with fear, before Mr. Murphy will dislodge from my face, taking with it strings of reddened and white flesh which will expand forever similar to bubblegum. Sorry for the gross depiction, it's how my mind works, I suppose I am a little gross when it comes to specific areas, although you can't put down a good horror movie.

IT IS good to hear you have no Watson... I have no Sherlock, so perhaps it is something we can work toward because you seem cool, I suppose... I don't know. Plus, why do you reckon you would be a crappy partner; every cop show has a crappy partner... yeah, that sounded wrong, it didn't seem as lovely as it did in my head, forget the reference. I am sure you'd make a good detective. And the cheek, I cannot believe you called me a secretary, that is insulting but oddly funny at the same time. I can't understand why I am smiling at the letter beneath me as I print this, but for the first time, I think I found someone who shares the same humor, well I reckon.

AS TO THE QUESTION, am I jock, I don't believe so. I suppose I am if you are one of those shy kids who keep to themselves, then I guess you could say I am a jock. I'm not mean or anything; sportspeople are given a bad reputation when it comes to Hollywood, I promise we are not all like that... and I use "*ALL*" for emphasis. Perhaps every 3 out of 5 people are stable, promise.

From what I can tell, you seem cool enough to be able to pass the ball with. I wouldn't mind if you joined in on a game. If you are no good at the start, I can help you get better, I remember the first time I started Baseball, I was so clumsy. I played Lacrosse last year, and I dropped it this year because I have too many sports to contend with. My mom said I was beginning to look a little sickly because I was constantly going and having no downtime, so I decided to drop one... Yeah, I wasn't very popular for doing that. Except my couch understood, it was great; he even said if I wanted to retry next season that a spot is opened for me above newbies. Perhaps when the couple of weeks are up, the two of us could meet up and toss a football back and forth or play catch. I'll start with the basics if you wanna learn. I don't know why I am offering to teach you or if you even want to, it just seemed like a natural thing to do. Sorry again.

True you made me smile, and I suppose it means we are getting on okay then. The Clarinet, I hear is hard to learn, although there is this dude across from me in-band who plays Clarinet, and he always tells me it's hard to play the instrument with his braces. Do you have braces? If you do, I hope it's not too difficult, and I'm sure you sound fantastic.

For your question, what instrument do I play, I play the piano. I have been playing for about six, maybe seven years. I like it because it gets me away from sports, even though I love sports. I feel alive when I am running with a ball in my hand on a field.

Except, nothing entirely competes with good music that makes you tingle inside. As far as a movie dude goes, I don't think I would call myself an enthusiast. I have a standard film collection, Netflix, and whatnot.

Winters get long, and I catch up on a lot of junk I missed out on in summer. In the summertime, I am never indoors, but you know... in winter everything is reduced. So, music and film pass the hours for me. As for games, I play a little bit of everything, mostly online stuff with friends though. We like to group up and do things together, it is always better with more people, and with folks, you know. How about you, are you a movie guy?

Thanks for the wishes of Basketball, I hope so too, I need everything to go well. I did write back to you; I kept my promise lol. As for Watson, we'll see, it sounds too... too geeky lol.

FROM,

James Bond... AKA - Watson - A Glorified Secretary

ENTRY #6

To Mr. James Bond or Glorified Secretary,

I AM WRITING to authenticate the unique package of God's almighty power you have sent has been received. PS. Could you post an instruction handbook because one did not arrive with the cargo, furthermore considering I'm all about saving the planet and recycling, I don't want to have to wire back the delivery in order to get a manual, only for you to ship it back to me?

There exists some commonality as to what you have said; I too believe sleep is more beneficial than losing it. On the contrary, I reason everybody would agree with you that rest is increasingly essential. I have to say I would kiss the feet of the person who invented the bed. Oh and the dude who created a pillow. They have made my life so much more comfortable; moreover, if I ever met them, I'd be sure to let them know.

However, seldom it is unavoidable in life, the reason I hold good grades and excel with most of my studies is that I put the work in, if you don't put the performance in it'll never happen. I do agree to some of the rules they settle are a bit ridiculous, including your interpretation of the "*government*" or "*school board*" fits the bill. I would not beg to differ because I imagine it is entirely accurate, only on the downside if it weren't for school I don't think I'd know how to do basic Math or English. I deem classwork as if it were a sport. Your life resembles to revolve around sports and not that it is a bad thing or anything. Except what appears important to you, is not significant to me, but what is essential to me, is not important to you.

I reckon it makes the world a more inviting place and more diversified. It would be a dull, boring home to be living if every *Tom, Dick*, and *Harry* were the same. I have no problem sitting down every day, day after day, doing homework for more than 40 minutes, as you have pointed out. Despite, if I were to try sports, I would highly doubt I'd do 30 minutes of physical education.

And who knows? I might be even able to bend spoons with my brain waves. Don't underestimate the power of a geek, though you're in safe hands because I don't probe anybody, so that is something.

Cursing is not an overly huge deal with me. If you find it to be more natural and beneficial from your standpoint point of view, then swear all you want. Personally, though, on a side note, I don't curse a lot.

My mom often says, "*it does not become of you*," when I speak some bad language.

Except, bad language is not a common occurrence for me, nine times out of ten, it is usually associated with something that I find frustrating. For example, if I've worked on a science project for hours on end and then find out that I've arranged the wrong section that is when I will unleash the mighty foul expressions. I reckon it passes to everyone, that we end up doing something wrong when we're not listening because our minds are so filled with the nonsense teachers give out, our own personal dilemmas, as with society as a whole. I guess the further we delve into the eventuality the more complicated and less human we become. I'm going slightly off track here; therefore, I'll go back to my original point. Cursing is not something I do.

As for your invite in roasting a teacher, I would be on board with that. I have never done or said anything like this before, so this is out of context. There are some nice teachers out there; not all teachers are corrupt. I don't know why we're even talking about teachers being incredibly mean. Correct Mr. Murphy looks like he's gonna have at you, I did find it amusing how you described him. Essentially, I was envisioning it; the first thing that came to mind was, of course, a cheesy horror flick where a poor fool's face comes away like grated stringy cheese. I like horror movies they're kinda cool, do you prefer older or newer horror movies, you can't beat John Carpenter's films.

AYE, I have no Watson, it could be something we could work towards, plus I'll start preparing an exemplary objective test. I can't guarantee an offer, but you will go to the top of my list on my desk. Also, I will ensure that you get the place.

Err... And yeah, the crappy partner bit was a bit... Crappy if I can say that much. Thankfully I'd didn't take it to heart, and I am in a good mood, so that's water under the bridge. About the caveat, you're right, every cop show does have a crummy partner or one who kind of does their own business. But it's ironic that one person ends up making a significant breakthrough in the case so... Value your crappy partner.

I put it lightly about Watson; a glorified secretary is not something to turn down so quickly. Everybody knows a great detective or brain needs personal filing carbineer. I believe the two of us share some humor and I think that is how we are possibly getting on for the moment. It's good to be able to laugh at our little jokes. Plus, they haven't gotten out of hand for us to feel personally insulted. Consequently, if you like, let's keep it up.

I also assumed you were a jock, well not in the traditional sense, but I did have an inkling. After all, you sound like you get along with most people and well, you play sports, and a lot of it, which I will assume will become one of your main influences during high school. Possibly collage.

To your question "am I one of the shy kids," I assume I am, except I guess I'm not. You see, I don't fit inside a group that says shy or not shy. To be honest, I don't believe I have a peer group in school. I'm like my own wolf sort of deal, and I suppose it's okay, but sometimes it gets lonely. It's helpful to know not everyone in the jock social group is not a complete psycho, no offense. Thus, the probability of meeting three out of five people is an excellent winning number, considering I don't want to meet the other two of the five, although I'm going to hold you to that statistic.

For passing the ball, it sounds like a cool thing to do, I don't how you'd feel about me playing though, I don't presume you'd fancy playing with me if I got on a court. Furthermore, it's formidable that you are willing even to teach me; most people would not have the patience for such a thing. Especially a stranger.

It sounds like you're going to be a regular All-Star

throughout high school and perhaps college, you seem to have an interest in every spot there is by the looks of it. Nonetheless, moms know best, you should listen. Keeping your health is more important than trying to satisfy the team, I hope you resemble a little healthier or at least feel it. It's nice to know that you have left a lasting impression on the people you have come in contact with that they are willing to give you a second chance when you're ready to go at it again. Concerning me, I wish I knew such generous benefits, but I don't, I guess teachers are somewhat lenient. Only, I'd like to be looked up to, or a little bit admired at least some time within my life by my peers. I might take you up the offer for learning but... I surmise that it is an assumption for another day.

THE CLARINET IS REASONABLY hard to play. I've been playing the instrument for about four years, and yes, I do have braces which it is slightly weird now. Though I don't find it too difficult to perform the clarinet with a pair of train tracks, they didn't get in the way because all you're doing is blowing into the mouthpiece. Maybe I'm a little more self-conscious than I give myself credit for, reasonably I am a bit better than I give myself appraise for.

It would be funny to know that the two of us are in the same band class, and then to find out we are talking to each other in real life. It would be highly amusing to recognize that I am the guy with the braces, including you are the guy who plays the piano over in the corner which ironically when I was in the band class, there was a kid who played the piano, and he was pretty good actually. No idea if it's you, however, if you did play the piano for six years than I could assume that the kid who was playing the piano was playing for quite a while because he was pretty good.

I know right music makes you consider stuff that you cannot quite think of concerning anything else. It doesn't matter what language it is in or what it is regarding, music is a universal language, and it brings people together regardless of race, ethnic background or beliefs. Every emotion has a reaction, and experiencing that emotion has a beautiful response.

Too bad you're not a movie enthusiast. I play a lot of games although mostly solo player because I don't have many friends to play with online. Except, for the few that I do play with online, I don't really know them. I have a couple of friends but not a lot, therefore, if I have any friends, they are virtual ones. I'm a geeky guy, so it is in my arsenal to own at least a couple hundred films and a couple hundred games. I do like going outdoors in summer, yet there's just something about sitting down in the evenings in the middle of vacation and playing a game on your phone or pulling out an old Nintendo DS and going at it like the early days.

You're welcome, and I assume it will go well. Anyway, later.

From,
    Sherlock

ENTRY #7

To Sherlock,

OKAY, okay, okay... You may call me Watson. It looks to be a topic of discussion for every single one of our conversations as so far. Plus, it makes essential sense that you have a Watson considering your Sherlock. Can I possibly be the next best candidate? So, you tell me where and when I sign up for this test or whatever you call it. I'll be ready for it. And it is good to know that you got my package without it having further repercussions. I am sorry that no user guidebook came with the product, I'm afraid to inform you, no such document has been created. Therefore, you will have to contact customer support which, I might sadly have to say has never existed either so, follow that up by a quick Google search.

FURTHERMORE, of course, there is some sense to what I'm saying sleep is sleep... There is no denying that it holds more beneficial value than anything else that a teacher can say and correct, I have nothing against teachers. Though I do have a little bit of the cold stigma at the moment for Mr. Murphy because he's the one that got me into trouble and well... No offense but I wouldn't have to sit down and do this, if not for him. Not that the time spent talking to you has been bad.

If anything, I am enjoying our letters. Every day when I come into school, the box at the top of the class is the first place I go to see if I've received a reply. I have to say you respond quite quickly added; I'm finding it hard to keep up. I apologize if my responses are sluggish, but as I've probably mentioned, I do have a lot on my plate. Now why did I say anything about a dish, it's almost lunch currently, and now I'm hungry.

Anyhow, beds, on the other hand, are fantastic but I don't believe I'd warrant enough will power to go and kiss someone's feet. I find this weird for some particular reason because perhaps I don't think I'm one for showing public displays of affection quite easily.

I understand what you mean by putting work and effort in, and I do I put a lot of effort into past times I am passionate about. From what you have mentioned, I suppose, I could put some more time into developing myself outside of those areas. I admire what you said about what classwork means to you, as sports means to me. I believe it's like one of those things when you do it so much it becomes as rational as breathing and you can't exist without it. I never said that school is a waste of time; I'd happily applaud every teacher who has tried to better me, applied effort in coaching me and has stuck around with me even though I may not be the brightest student in the class.

. . .

THE REALM WOULD SURELY BE boring if everybody were the same, so I'll agree with you on that. Since everybody is different, that is how we have so many options. If everybody were identical, then I don't think there would be many options. Tom, Dick, and Harry... lol, you seem to have a way with one-liners which I like, oddly because they're quite blunt.

AND OKAY, I think I am going to keep my distance now considering you said that you could bend spoons. It's even weirder now since you noted, you don't probe humans. It makes it sound very alien and sci-fi cheesy.

PHEW... Good to know. I tend to cuss quite a bit, but it's not for the act of being macho or lit, it's mainly due to being honest. To be honest, my mom doesn't like me swearing either, but sometimes it just comes out, and I can't help it. It sounds like your mom knows what she's talking about and while I figure my mom has the same temperament; except I don't really listen to her all that much when it comes to my language. When I do cuss, it's not usually for the lack of being frustrated I typically cuss about everything because it adds emphasis to everything. For instance, I'll give you an example because I think it makes me sound more you know like me. Instead of saying, the road is long, I'll say, it's one long ass road. Still, it's not that much of a swear word, except sometimes mom gets crabby about me using such exemplifies.

. . .

So, you feel the same way, too, when it comes to technology and the way human development is going. It's scary to think that when I was younger I would go missing for hours playing out in the sunshine and then when I look at my little brother playing on an iPad it's sad. The little dude spends all day when he comes in from school on the iPad, occasionally breaking to do his homework, followed by dinner, where he will disappear back to the device, only to have a shower before bedtime, if mom gets lucky.

I believe we're going to get along just fine if you think John Carpenter's movies are lit. Do you think he's the best horror director there is? The new director James Wan is a pretty cool guy as well, he has revamped the face of horror, and I am pleasantly awaiting the new productions he puts his hand to.

AND YEAH, I apologize about the crappy cop thing. I wasn't thinking when I was composing it, but I didn't want to scribble it out because it would look messy and, I didn't have all that much time to rewrite the letter. I'm relieved you took it in a light spirit and didn't get upset by it. I didn't mean for it to come off as harsh as I did. It's just as I said, I'm pretty honest, and I don't think that fits well with some people.

Question... Do jocks have the traditional sense? I'm not sure what you are implying just because I get on well with people and have friends. I'm traditionally a jock. I reckon anybody who has friends and plays sports can equally, not be considered as a jock. I could say that I'm heading in that direction which I guess is okay but, if I want to fit in, I have to lead in that direction if you get my drift. Plus, I promise that not every person who plays physical sports is not a psycho. So, you're in safe hands. I'm not sure if you're trying to elude me in understanding that I'm going to be more popular than I am now probably, but that is not my primary concern. I don't aspire to quote and have everybody know me or have whoever' chase after me; I want to play for the fun of it.

WHEN I STARTED FEELING MORE tired and weaker, that is when I took my step back, but I'm glad I did it now when I think about it because I feel a lot better. I remember every day when I got in from school when I did not have practice; I'd sleep for two hours when I got home. When I came back from training when I did have to stay out after school hours, by the time I got home, I literally had no energy left. I was missing days when my friends wanted to hang out, and all I could tell them was that I was too tired all the time. It was not fair on anyone, and of all people, it was not for me. I think for most of my sports teams, my coaches expected me to perform well, and my team members did so too. Most will say something if I have a crappy record or if on that feeling if it has consequences. Sometimes it's incredibly hard to live up to other people's expectations; furthermore, I feel like that's what I'm doing most of the time. I do like what I do, I'm not complaining here, it's just sometimes it would be nice to be able to take a step back and relax for a minute. Of all the coaches I've met, my lacrosse coach is the best. After this season with my track in basketball, I might go back to Lacrosse because I'm itching to get back on the field.

You're not saying what I think you're saying though are you? That would be incredibly weird if you are the kid sitting across from me with the braces who plays a clarinet. I never considered it before when you said clarinet because you said you left and right... There was a kid who split from band practice as well who also played a clarinet, but that was last year, and I'm not sure if that was you, but I can't honestly remember the kid. I'm sorry if that was you. From what I recall the dude was pretty cool actually. Or perhaps it could be the fact that you are in the other band class which I've never set foot in so what's the odds that another piano player who looks or seems similar to me is on a piano next door.

I never said this to anyone before, but the reason I joined the marching band was that I liked music. I still do about sad and cheerful melodies. Do you feel the same way about music as I do? Touching things that cannot be provoked when doing other hobbies makes the magic of songs special, and it conveys a lot of understanding and emotion. I have heard that some people go without listening to music. I don't believe how their life is interesting. Sure you can have a bit of both worlds', but no music means you're not a happy person and considering every person nearly listens to it all the time, they understand how extraordinary it is. Except for the small minority, only a select few will truly understand what music is.

I'M sorry to hear you don't have many friends, and I'd be happy to be your friend here or in real life if you want to. I'm not saying it just for pity either because you genuinely sound like a cool person; therefore, I'm open to making a new friend. I don't think I have many virtual friends, in fact, I think everyone I play with online I know, so there's that. Second, I don't hate you or anything like that, or there's no weird stigma because you like games and films. I love video games and movies also so, no pressure.

May I ask why you like being a lone wolf. You mention it; what does it entail? Do you ever get lonely; find it hard to express yourself when no one is there to listen? If I pried too much, I'm sorry, and I hope this doesn't make things weird.

Anyway, see you

From,
   Watson... Agent has terminated.

ENTRY #8

To Watson,

Yes, you may take the occupation of a friend, and partner in crime since it appears to be the abundant show of interest. It saddens me to learn you have no such implementation; may I propose that your company adapts, as they say, the customer is perpetually right. I would not have paid for the parcel if I possessed knowledge of intentional manufacturer infringement, where the seller cuts corners for-profit and lower production costs. It is a mockery and insult that you don't supply customer support for dedicated consumers, MORE or less tell me to "google" it and sort it myself.

Onward for now; to pass my exemplary objective test, you must answer the following questions.

1. How good are your coffee brewing skills?

2. What do you do say to, getting covered in personal sticky notes?
3. Sometimes I get lonely, how good is your singing voice? Can you teach me how to yodel?
4. Do you make badass sandwiches, I love a good ol' sandwich?
5. If you are falling to your death, do you scream, cry, or pee a little?

IF YOU REACH the requirements above, you may fill the position. Plus, I have no quarrels about hibernation, I do love the rest when I can afford to switch my brain off. Unfortunately, there is not a whole lot for me to do, all I do is school and home, after that, I am kind of dull to be around. Consequently, sleep is a beautiful thing to break up the whole glum glamorous lifestyle of being somewhat a loser.

SORRY TO HEAR Mr. Murphy got you into hot water. Personally, I don't have classes with him, but I do know of him. I have listened to the stories and ridiculous conditions he expects from his students. I understand where you are coming from. However, it didn't sting in the slightest bit. I can assume that you are just a little bit peeved off because you were being made do something you do not entirely want to do. I reckon everybody who has had to do something they are not happy about doing, will have never done it if they were not forced to do it. I have been in those circumstances, I have had to adapt to when things go wrong, and well... here I am, having somewhat come out on the far side of said event thankful in some way or form. Therefore, I get where you are coming from, I am starting to think that not all sports people are "*dicks*." Sorry for the crude language, only that is what I have been conditioned to believe or from personal experience.

As for kissing someone's feet, I agree I think I went too far, I don't deem I would smooch someone's rotten, stinky feet, not even for a million dollars. Although there are things I wish I could fix with a million dollars, a friend would be one of them. Ironically, I know that friends cannot be bought with money... except it always seems like the general premise when you have it, and the illusion of being accepted is comforting when you have capital, but not fulfilling.

I never stated that you didn't put in work to better yourself. I am passionate about specific hobbies too. I don't have the heart to do them anymore, and well with that, there is a certain extent to what I'll do considering I find it hard to fit in. I reckon we feel the same about school and recreational life. It is something that you do naturally without second guessing without you doing it. I figure now that you mention it, I could try and improve my ability around people. I am not the most prominent people person, not anymore, anyway. It's not that I hate people or anything, it's just that I find people tend to judge me rather quickly, and I don't like that. I have been sentenced all my life, though I reckon it's nothing compared to what they are presumably pondering now. Anyway, I don't want to get into a sob story, so I'll continue forward.

I like people who are different, I don't think I'd settle for mediocrity, there is much more on offer from the local cashier down in Walmart alone, than just to confine yourself to that one person. I wouldn't say I'm naturally the funniest person in the world, however, if you like it, I'll sure keep it up because I'm not putting on an act.

EVEN IF I may be able to bend spoons, it is not my only psychic ability. I also may be hiding in plain sight. The next time you see another dude with a bagel with a hole in the middle of it, who appears to be probing it, run the other way, that's our signal telling you that we are aliens. I assume I do sound a little sci-fiy, I guess I'm a little into the 1980s flicks; thus, I think it's nothing new to talk about.

YEAH, it's all right, good to know that you don't do it just for the sake of doing it. Many people do it in our peer group, to sound superior, or more or less hyped. In all honesty, I think my mother would actually applaud me for using some foul language because it's not every day I'd use such vocabulary. It's funny to imagine that I would probably get away with it if I went off on a tangent with lousy language once or twice, but probably not any more than that. Oh, and I understand how you mean that you add emphasis to everything using a particular word. If it's a long-ass road, it's a long-ass road.

I WOULDN'T BE one to defy technology, because that would be going against my roll considering I'm a geek of sorts. Technology is sort of my mojo, so why would I say it is downright unnerving. Sure, it is a little freaky to notice that some kids are using software more excessively these days, and I think parents should be a bit more conservative about how their children use said devices. I know when I was growing up, my mother probably wouldn't have allowed me to use a computer to the quantity young kids use electronics today. You said that you are naturally a physical person so instead of watching your brother sit, playing on an iPad, which you have stated is sad to see, why don't you do what typically comes to you and take him out and pass some ball or something. I know it's not my place to dictate, but it just seems like the natural thing to do considering, if I were any good at that, and I had a brother that's what I'd do.

JOHN CARPENTER IS a legend of course, but I don't believe he is the best horror director ever. He is up there with Wes Craven, George A. Romero, Tobe Hooper, and Alfred Hitchcock. In case you don't know who, Alfred Hitchcock is, he's that guy who created all those sick films in the 1950s about birds that have nothing better to do other than perch highly on children's climbing frames and shit. Or: a lunatic who dresses up in his mother's clothes, spies on women before eventually stabbing them to death in the shower dressed as his dear old mother. The best saved for last has to be Rear Window, there is something creepier about the dude next door who is spying on you using a telephoto lens. If the act of murder is not grotesque enough, spying on someone without their knowledge is presumably even creepier than the killing itself. Anyway, I think I've gone on a bit too long about movies, so I don't want to bore you. Moving on. I don't believe John Carpenter is the best director of horror. Though the genre has died somewhat in the last couple of years, I can finally say I have some faith in the genre being revived by a newbie director called James Wan. Horror can never be solely one person, it is a group effort.

. . .

Hey, the cop things' behind us don't worry about it, although considering your pondering partner material, it's good to notice that you didn't scribble it out and changed your mind abruptly.

Well, in the traditional sense, at least 90% of all jocks are high up on the popularity chain. You probably have more friends alone this year of high school, than I have ever had in my entire life. I'm not saying in any way that you are a traditional jock. I'm just saying that in general, it seems to be the case. People who consider themselves energetic and sporty, typically have more friends than the average person who might be a bit of a loner. Make friends all you want, the more, the merrier, if it pleases you then head in that direction. Just I know it's weird, but don't forget about me if you become big all of a sudden. I know it's a little odd considering we've only met, but it seems like I enjoy talking with you.

I hope you are feeling better, a lot of guys around our age don't seem to be able to take no for an answer. A lot of people believe since we are young that we are the healthiest and have no mental, physical, or any other extremities. The truth in it all is that you should take care of yourself no matter what and if anybody pushes you in a direction that you don't wish to go, you should take a step back. It sounds like you suffer from chronic fatigue or something. Usually, you have to take supplements or something in order to make it through the day, but ironically most Americans from what I've researched over the coming years, supplement it using coffee. Plus, you have no idea what it means to live up to other people's expectations. If you understand it, then I guess both of us have something in common. I don't correctly tick all the boxes for people my age, not anymore. Sigh...

I LOVE your philosophy about music, it is right, a matter of fact, a small minority will only understand what it truly means. Just like a small minority of scientists who will only ever know what we are, no much more or less than what it is we can convey or do.

I highly doubt I was the kid in your music class playing the clarinet. Usually, people tend to miss me so if you are pretty popular in music class playing the piano which most pianists are, considering it is a significant instrument and is under their possession, I don't think someone in your position would've even noticed me. Then again in the odd notion, you did see me, then I thank you for regarding me if it was indeed in fact me. May I ask what grade you are in so that I can help distinguish whether it truly was me in your class or not. Finding how we are on the topic of music, what musician breaks you and fulfills you?

I BELIEVE that is all I have to say today. I have also probably been a bit short and rough, I hope you don't hold it against me. Till next time.

FROM,
   Sherlock

ENTRY #9

To Sherlock,

Yes, you are awesome, thank you so much, I won't disappoint you, Mr. Holmes. I will be the best quote unquote secretary you have ever had since whenever your first book was composed. I wish to apologize and say that I agree that it is uncool that our company does not have a customer returns policy. Unfortunately, since I am not HQ, I will pass on your proposal, and I will pray that they will implement your devised plan and adapt our operating criteria to make it more beneficial for the customer.

I have to say you got a chuckle out of me with your questions. I was expecting real inquiries for some weird reason. I don't know why, but that was just that. I didn't think you'd take it as a joke, though inherently you were. Nevertheless, I had a good laugh at your expense, and I thank you for that. So, as to the questions outlined in the text below, I will answer them.

1. How good are my coffee brewing skills? – Let's just assume that it is legendary for the moment. I pour half a container of coffee, and then I add a sweet mixture of hot boiling water. From there it either turns out like tar or a good cup of Joe. I'll let you decide when you actually try it, but I want to make it officially clear if you die from ingesting my poison, I will take no part in it, and you've been warned.
2. What do I say to being covered in sticky notes? As odd as it may sound that appears to be appealing. How many people can say that they've been covered like a shredded chicken, or like the guys from Home Alone after they've gone through the obstacle with all the feathers from the pillows? Rightly that is what I imagine, it is what I picture in mind. If we have an office together, and I walk into your personalized detective suite covered in stickies of all different luminous colors. I'd really light up the room now wouldn't I? Then somewhere from that mess all across my body, I look down and noticed that your 2:30 appointment was over an hour ago, and I didn't call in to tell you that the person has been sitting in the lobby for the last hour. Somehow, I find it amusing.
3. Unfortunately, I sing like an Irish Banshee, I cannot say that my singing voice is spectacular or anything to be duly noted. I must suggest if you wish to hear me singing I can try to get you a nice little tune or two going, which will probably make your ears bleed. Then again, that is entirely up to you if you wish to wear air defenders when

I start my singing. I might know a little country, a little bit of pop and some Tina Turner but that's about it. As for yodeling, yes that's not gonna happen. I'm not reenacting the yodeling kid from Walmart. I guess if I did presumably try, I'd cough up blood because it is so hard to do, but then again why did I make this all so dark all of a sudden? I reckon my mind is twisted.

4. Do I make good sandwiches? To your amazement, I do. Not that you will ever get one because you know Sherlock has to make his own just because everybody has a peculiar taste. Plus, that is not something I do. I'm supposed to do your filing work, not your BLT. Except, I guess I could let you in on the secret recipe of my lunches, and you can make me a sub; then we will all live in a sandwich land, and everybody will be so happy eating sandwiches.

5. Last but not least, what would be my initial reaction of falling to my death? Most certainly I would pee a little, cry all of my descent on the way down. I even scream the moment I get close to the edge of a cliff. I'm not a fan of heights, so let's keep that between the two of us, and never endanger each other when heights are concerned. If I was on a high building and you were climbing, and you fell, dangling hanging on by one arm. Well then, I'd say adios. I ain't going nowhere near that ledge.

So, will you tell me how I did? Did I pass the test, or am I blindly addicted to the hope that I will be accepted by your excellence? Therefore, let's just agree that both of us love to sleep in general, because whenever I can get it, I never want it to end.

As for Mr. Murphy, I'm over it... I think. You're lucky that you don't have any classes with him because he's a right dickhead... Whatever you do, please don't show this to your teacher or otherwise I could get in further trouble for even calling a faculty member such a ludicrous word. Truth be told yes, he does expect a little bit more from your average student when such a thing is not possible. Again, I'm sorry if that stung a bit of the reference concerning Mr. Murphy and how I am stuck participating in this program. Then again, I surmise I'm not the only one considering everybody around me is writing letters.

When I look to my left and both right, I wonder if the people who they are talking to is like you and me. Just how far did they get on communicating alone. I believe we've gotten off to a great start and everything seems to be looking up. I'm optimistic about the future here, I hope you are too. Even though it's turning out to be beneficial in the long run for my grades, I'm delighted I'm making a new friend. Let's scratch the idea of getting a grade. I think the bond we are starting to develop is a lot stronger than any grade can give.

I'M NOT sure what brought upon your interpretation of *all jocks* to be *dicks*. I'm sorry if, in the past, my social group has had an adverse effect on you. I promise though if you were hanging out with me, it wouldn't be like that. I'd treat you like any other person I know. Furthermore, I'm sorry if the reason you have had to adapt and change your lifestyle just to fit in was that of someone like me apparently. Genuinely I think I am a nice guy, I don't mistreat anybody. So maybe if you could just try and accept that not every sporty person is a dickhead and I am not out to get you or anything, then that would be good.

MONEY CAN BUY NICE THINGS, but yeah right, cash cannot buy a good friend, trust, and loyalty or happiness. I remember I watched a documentary a while back... I know: don't judge, I watch documentaries. Now, on the contrary, I don't watch them all the time, but just so you know, I do like getting a bit of information every so often. Anyhow, I was saying I saw this addition about how people in America are faring when it comes to happiness and the work-life. It finds that people who tend to have more capital in their bank accounts, more of the luxurious things in life, seem to be generally obnoxious. Where are people who have a lump sum of money to live from, but not entirely rich, and neither are they in the middle-class section of the socioeconomic level? They tend to be somewhat within the happiest because they are experiencing a bit of the best of both worlds. Ideally, the people who have the least are also the most content. The ones who want more or less are typically the saddest.

In most cases, many of these people who have come a long way have had to grow and open such positions where money was not always a common element. My family is okay; I suppose with money. We are comfortable, I'd reckon we are more than adequate. My dad is a lawyer, we have comfort that we did not know we had about 10 years ago, and that makes all the difference. However, I would not say that we are extremely rich, or anything like that but I don't think I would want to be because I'm happy where I am.

. . .

I'm sorry perhaps I misinterpreted what you actually were saying. I'm sorry if I got my wording wrong or stated that you weren't passionate. It's just you made it sound like that you don't do anything. You're either not excited enough about it, or you're either a little nervous to even try it. I can tell you that being scared is an integral part of anything when you're starting from scratch. The way I look at it is that we're only here once, so why waste all the time in the world when you don't have all the time in the world.

Seems like just yesterday I was sucking on my thumb and running around in diapers, now I'm like I don't know, trying to figure out the whole dating game and stuff like that. I tell you, man it is difficult. Of course, I wouldn't let anybody know that because you know if I was saying I wanted to date them... well... I'd try to be smooth. I guess at least trying is better than not even giving it a chance. Except for heights you can skip that part, I ain't doing that.

TYPICALLY, when I run into people who have a different outlook on life, I welcome them with open arms. The world would get boring so quickly and so fast if everyone were the same and to be honest, I don't think I'd want to live if everyone were the same. Who wants to go around like a motionless zombie all the time when there is better experiences and things to see and awesome stuff to do.

ABOUT YOUR PSYCHIC ABILITY; yeah, you stay well away from me... Bending spoons is not something the average human can do so away-away. That is unless your intellectual capacity is actually grabbing the spoon from the top and the bottom and twisting it with your bare hands. Good to know the tip has been noted, and any time I see another dude with a bagel with a hole in it and his finger in the center, I will run the other way.

Just a random thought which will probably make you chuckle but my father calls ring doughnuts, "*donuts with a less fatting center.*" I don't know why, but I always found it funny, and I've never corrected him on it. I think we all have our little quirks, that is one of his.

Good on you choosing the alternative route against foul language. You were really serious about your mother applauding you for using bad language? Your mom sounds wicked... Not in a bad way, I mean like wicked awesome. If I were to do that, I'd probably get a slap across the back of the head by my dad or something you know for using such context. And hey the long-ass abbreviation is my thing: you find your own Sherlock. I thought of it first so away-away.

You know you're a genius, I have thought about bringing my little brother out to play outside to get him off the computer.

Except for the number one thing I always hear when I bring him out to play ball is, "*do we have to do this.*" Or, "*I'm tired.*"

Parents should take a little bit more consideration when they are buying their kids electronics. I presume now these days it's considered an integral part of life where parents need to buy their kids stuff in order for the kids to keep up with their peer group. I reckon an iPhone would be like rookie cards back in the day.

That said I thought you would've said John Carpenter's a legend. I know most of the names you mentioned on the list, and I know Alfred Hitchcock. I'm not exactly stupid, you know. Besides the points, I did find your little interpretation about how you listed off Psycho, Rear Window, and The Birds. Dear old mother had me in stitches.

I can assume that it is a creepy thing to have a guy staring at you through a telescope or camera. I can imagine that is something that happens in real life, and well I hope I've never been spied on. As for the new director James Wan, isn't he the guy who directed The Conjuring.

I'm sorry for having friends okay, I mean I can't correctly do anything about it if people just want to talk to me. I can't say, "*here I don't want to talk to you because I'm not allowed to make friends.*"

Can I ask why you like bashing all the jocks? It's like you have vengeance or something and we're not all like that bad. I'm trying to be as nice as I can here, so can you at least try to be accommodating. I might have some friends, but of all of the people that I'm surrounded by, I probably only trust one or two people so theoretically, I've only one or two friends. And I can assume that everyone else has the same.

I think music is neat, only some will really get it. I believe that's the mystery question of life. "*Who we are, and what is our real purpose for being here.*" The other ideology is, "*are we alone in this universe.*"

Plus, don't be so quick to brush off the concept of you being the other kid there might be a possibility that you are. Who knows? Do you have blonde hair; that might narrow the suspect pool. I'm beginning to make a bit of a mental image as far as I can remember. I only need a gazillion other things down, and then I might be able to make a computer-generated model of you in my head. Okay, I heard that too... it's creepy.

You consider a piano a significant instrument, I suppose it is a big ask when you're told to play a specific event, but I think of it as another instrument. I don't set out to be cool by playing, I just do it.

Anyway, I think I should go... I think I've written enough, and could you please maybe try and stop making it sound like all jocks are evil. I ensure we're really not. Oh, and eh... I'm in ninth grade. How about you; what grade are you in?

RIGHT, well see-ya

FROM,
   Watson

ENTRY #10

To Watson,

I BET your jumping and jiving today since it is Friday. I acknowledge I'm going to miss you over the weekend. I suspect whatever it is you get up to it is better than whatever I arrange to do. I can visualize what I am going to do already; sit in and observe the world go by and possibly play some PlayStation 4. Or alternatively, I might travel on down to the swimming pool and go floating. I hate having to bring my little cousin with me, she gets in the way, and all I desire to perform is to swim without any restrictions. Thank God for lifeguards because they can keep an eye on her most of the time. All I have to do is get her from point A to point B. The distance of my home is a little less than a miles' walk from the aquatics center.

I overheard the Tigers have a lacrosse rivalry on Saturday, well... tomorrow I mean, but I was wondering if you're going to go to the game to watch it. No idea why I mentioned it, I just know that you like lacrosse, therefore, I figured you'd be one person to go watch your teammates play.

Anyway, on to your letter, I know I'm awesome, I was born awe-inspiring. Except you have to look past all the blood and guts because deep down when I was born there was awesomeness there. I like your style quote, unquote secretary. I know you won't let me down, I'm assuming you will be an excellent correspondent. Plus, I'm also sorry about the things I said about jocks. I don't determine to be crude or cutting about your peer group; it's just stuff has happened in the past that I'm not at liberty to speak about right now. However, I am confident that you are different than the rest; I am sorry if I have offended.

I'm about to well up, that has to be the most joyous news I have received all week. Screwball industries are going to empower my devised plan and adapt their operating conditions to suit the customer who is always right.

Now let's get down to business... I had a quick gander over your answered question', now I have to say I am thoroughly impressed.

1. I would be more than happy to try out your legendary brewing skills, though now I'm a little skeptical since you mentioned that it could be poison. I have a magnificent brain, and I don't want any of that to go to ruin due to some sort of tar you make. Therefore, I reject the proposal to try your cup of Joe, I aspire to exist until old age.
2. I never concluded that sticky notes would be quite so loud if they were attached to another

person, but now that I perceive it, I look forward to witnessing the first human neon subject. Yes, please don't leave my occupants sitting in the front lobby for over an hour if they are expecting me. What sort of debauchery is that?

3. I have no idea what a banshee is, save I'm assuming it's something very screechy. I would be lying if I said I am not slightly puzzled and a little disappointed. I believed you'd have the voice of an angel, and you'd sing on a street corner to make ends meet when a case is currently idle on your desk. You may refrain from using the name Tina Turner again, I'm not a fan of her music. Still, you can't deny that Simply The Best is a grand jam or 9-to-5. How do we know her- she's old. That dark curdling vision of you coughing up blood from yodeling is enough to haunt me. Therefore, I cease on the concept of you ever yodeling.

4. It saddens me to realize that I will never get a sandwich made by your professional hands. After all, I am the higher rhetorically here, and you're my secretary, so present me a god damn sandwich... I'm kidding. Now that you mention it, Sandwichland would be utterly engrossing, let's build that world together on a server.

5. Well adios is not a nice thing to say. What if I'm holding the full basket of sandwiches or something like that and I slipped? They are our lifeline. Would you still let me fall to my demise? I can work and help you get over your fear of heights well... The trick shot here is trying, I didn't say I will, but I'll most definitely strive to

push you off the side of the cliff so that you can get your fear out of the way. I need a fearless man on my team, and I ain't got time for petty jitters.

SINCE YOU ANSWERED everything accordingly and as honestly as you possibly can, I would be delighted to say that you have passed my test. There is an empty desk in the cloakroom of my office. If you would like to take that work surface you may. A word of warning, however, there is about 10 years' worth of paperwork piled on top of it so have at it.

And yes, let's agree that both of us love to sleep; nothing is better than it. I admire how you called me your excellence. It preferably has: I don't know superior prose, I suppose. It kinda feels weird but yeah.

I RECKON I am lucky not to have Mr. Murphy considering most of my peers in my year have gotten him already. I'm in 10th grade, so therefore I can clarify I do not have Mr. Murphy. He does teach more than one class, so yeah. Relax I won't tell Mr. Scruples what you called his friend. Wouldn't it be funny to have a teacher with that name? I think it would be? I hope for the remainder of my time here that I don't end up with him. I have been shared some pretty ridiculous conditions from him by other students, and I hope I never have to endure him.

Same too, when I peer around currently as I pen this letter, everyone else is preoccupied with writing to their behalf. I presume it does raise the question to have other duos got on as well as we have got on so far, as far. We are warming up quite nicely, and I think we've gotten some of the awkward stuff out of the way, you know the usual hellos and misinterpreted beginnings. You've no idea what that means to be called a friend. As I've said I don't have many so if you cross me as a friend now that I have yet to meet, then I deem that something.

I don't mean to be singling out anybody, only that has always been my case. I don't aim to imply you are like them, but I'll stop... sorry.

I GUESS you have stumbled onto something. I reckon it does look like that when half the time I am unwilling to try stuff... but it's just something you won't understand okay. I don't mean to be crabby or anything. I have things to deal with that most people don't have to deal with... So, if I drop the jocks being well... you know dicks thing. Can you cut the whole business that I am not passionate, and don't want to do anything? I am aware that being sad, hesitative, and joyous is a natural part of life. It's just my thing, okay... So, I won't mention anything about jocks being dicks again, if you lay off a little on the whole, "*have you got a dream... then seize it*," ideal.

I presume I have a different outlook on life, so if we were to meet in person, you owe me a hug. I won't forget, you know. I imagine it would be my mother's reaction to me using misused language. About four-five summers ago, she asked me to get angry to shout and curse, except I didn't, and I think she got more upset about it. I don't know why, she kept badgering on saying, "***** you must be holding a lot of anger and bitterness inside of you from what happened... Just show me you're angry about it. *Scream, yell, curse* the high-heavens."

Except I didn't, and I sat through the entire lecturing

and wished she finish up soon so I could be let go from captivity. Oh, and the five asterisks is my name, I know where not allowed use it, but she did say my name, so I decided to add it in to keep it authentic. Oh, and yeah, I guess the whole long-ass thing is your idea.

Gee... that is pretty sad to hear about, sorry. You see, if kids have a short attention span, I wonder what they will be like in another twenty years when their minds and sense of discipline has dwindled to nothing. Sometimes I wish I had a brother or sister to pass some time with. I am an only' child. Sometimes it gets lonely being by my lonesome. I spend a great deal of my time in the company of people who are not my friends. Only, if I had a brother or sister, who was younger than me, I'd love to be able to help them with homework, talk about their school day. Let them vent when they are upset or have their heart crushed by a girl or boy, whichever way they choose to go in life. I bet, however, as you said, iPhones are as valuable a commodity between our peer group more so than the likes of rookie cards of yesterday's obsession.

Ah and yes, I like sizing up things for what they are, and all I see from that turn of the century classic horror is a madman who likes the occasional dressing up. Though hey, each to one's own. Just if you end up wearing frock's and begin talking to yourself, let me know because I don't want to be the poor unfortunate soul in the next shower cubicle. Whereas with Rear Window, yes, the concept is creepy, they did an updated version of the movie in 2007, I believe called Disturbia. There is no way in hell anyone can say the film is it's own thing, it is almost a carbon-copy. Save to say, however, the adaption is a decent offering. Yes, James Wan is the guy and the genius behind The Conjuring series, as well as Insidious and Saw.

IT DOESN'T MATTER about the friend's thing... Alright... I didn't mean it earlier, okay. I don't know what I was talking about. It's just how can I not comment on it when you make it sound like you are really popular and I am not. Of course, I am going to be somewhat semi-jelly about it. I understand what you mean, and I don't expect you to have to say to someone that you can't talk to them because you can't be friends. It sounds like a lot of work being popular. Is that true? I work quite hard not to be noticed, and you perhaps strive in the other direction, although can you officially say it is grueling work. You're lucky you have one or two good friends. Sure, most people have two influential people in their lives they can trust, mine would be my mother. I know it is lame, though as I mentioned, I am not a hit with other teenagers. It's like I only show up to school, do the required lessons, and then disappear off the face of the world where other teenagers are considered. I asked my mom could I be homeschooled.

Ironically, she said, "you need to be around people your age."

Amen, that is the mystery, and I believe from storytelling, that is the only reasonable conclusion we can draw upon when we decide to contemplate life's more significant questions. In my mind, the bible is the best book ever written. The collection of stories that the book has amassed is enough to brainwash many people. The way I see it, there is nothing above us other than sky and the vast unknown, below: a planet with enough bodies to provide fresh fertilizer to stretch the entire globe, conjoined with rock and molten. A story is the only thing we have ever gotten right because, with the story, there is no such thing as right or wrong. We believe in our hearts, our minds more like considering the heart is a muscle, that story is all we know in order to fill in what's missing in our lives.

Well, I went deep, didn't I... I should leave it here. Class is about to finish, and I have to be ready to get out of the classroom ahead of everyone else considering folks will want to rush out the door. Please when you read this letter on Monday: tell me what your weekend was like.

Until Later,
    From,
    Sherlock

ENTRY #11

To Sherlock,

I CHOSE to stay behind after school let out, I know weird right. I'll miss chatting with you also; that is until Monday rolls around again. I have to say the teachers transfer the contents of the mailboxes daily and even on a Friday, that is what I call service because I received your note.

As with the end of your message, I can't quite say what the weekend has in store for me. I suspect I have some work to catch up on, and my dad requires me to begin searching for a summer job for when the semester finishes. Like I want to work; vacation time is to chill and soak up the sun. I wish I lived in California or something, they are lucky they get the lovely weather almost every day and then when it does rain, it is equally as unique. I have Basketball practice on the weekend, the coach decided to relocate it from a weekday to the weekend, so that is going to be great... eating up our weekend.

I hope that the practice goes well. Otherwise, I estimate I

might ask the coach to switch me around with one of the other players because I am not up to par. I would not be able to play comfortably and go home following a match and pretend everything is okay when I let the entire team down and myself. I'd rather let someone else fulfill the roll while I get back on track. I don't usually like allowing people to take my place in the world, just I guess its better than hearing my friends mouthing off to me how I screwed up, or possibly noticing them behind my back saying things.

Sounds like you get stuck with your cousin as I do get lumbered with my little brother.

Mom is like, "here, take Jordon with you..."

Like I need him to latch to me like the plague when my friends are about. I cannot do some of the more grown-up things due to him present. I have nightmares alone imagining what he'd say to my mom if he caught me doing something that he did not understand or thought I should be doing. Plus, he gets grumpy sometimes, and if he gets annoyed at me and rats me out for something petty, now that's just stupid.

AH, yes, thank God for lifeguards, they are ~~hot~~. I mean hospitable, they are fantastic when they let two people go down a slide or something... But yeah anyway my mom or dad usually drives me to the swimming pool. The last time I went with the boys, my friend Coren hit his head on the bottom of the pool, and he ended up with a nosebleed. We were not horsing around, but the dude that helped out was neat. The young man stood talking to us by the edge of the pool as we all huddled around my friend sitting on the tiled window pane. We hung around for a bit until Coren said it was okay to head off, and thank God he said it because it was starting to get cold. You know when you get out of warm water, and then the crisp air in the room begins to attack you, and your only reaction is to shiver well... Yeah, that's what happened. No idea why that seemed like something to tell, but I just thought it was.

Ah, and yes, the Tigers have a game tomorrow. What sort of question is that? Of course, I am going. They are my old team. I have to support them no matter what. After all, my little brother might end up on the same team, when he's old enough to drive any interest in sports. I'll never get the little doofus in my life; Jordon is good at Lacrosse and football, he's fast, faster than me. I could see him being a linebacker. Except he has no motivation.

Ah, yes, my messy, jumbled up job interview. I am surprised that I even got in at all. From what I have read, it could suggest you liked my previous reply comparing it to your response to the five questions you conducted to see if I was adequate.

Yes, I am humbly sorry for destroying the excitement you built up for wanting to taste my legendary brewing skills. However, just to clarify... I did say you could drink it, but it could be poisoned. After all, it is entirely up to you if you wish to do a risky deed after all. For me, if I saw my cup of Joe, I don't think I would even regard whether the coffee is like tar. I'd still helplessly sip it without considering whether the thing is poison or not. Funny ain't it? Wouldn't take a genius to eliminate me if I were King.

STICKY NOTES. Yeah, I reckon that would be quite bright like a neon sign. Kind of funny I guess, but yeah, I'd probably be one of those receptionists who consistently makes excuses, and always send your clients in late. Look at the bright side, you'll have plenty of free time on your calendar. If anything, you should be delighted to have such a caring and compassionate secretary who mopes around for most of the day and lets you relax. Well, the real reality in the entire situation is that I will be lying face down on the desk in the foyer.

To the best of my knowledge from what my father told me a couple years back. An Irish banshee is theoretically a fairy of varieties. It's usually a woman who's moderately old and who can be heard shrieking or groaning. Nonetheless, in most situations, when a banshee is discussed, its typically witnessed as a young woman, as a prospect for young men. The illusion is given that the sweet young singing girl is every man's dream. However, at nighttime, that is when her real horror shines through. She can be seen nestling beneath the trees, shrouded in cloaked garments, lamenting and caressing her veiled face, even crying. Anybody who is caught out with her during the night, has said that she can shape shift to some sort of degree, and the lovely singing turns from sweet blissful melody to bitter crying and squawking. There is also the adage that if it is a quiet night, and you hear screeching over the hillside: someone of your immediate family is bound to certain death.

PERHAPS I DO HAVE the voice of an angel, I just, I never really tried. I reckon I could give it a whirl and see do I deafen anybody. No problem I'll refrain from mentioning Tina Turner again. She does have some good jams. Now I have been saddened by your statement, I was looking forward to helping you yodel.

As much as life is full of disappointments, what is life when you really look at it; it's a piece of shit ain't it. I presume there are a lot of sadder things to miss out on than a professional handmade sandwich by my hands. But I agree with you... Sandwichland would be utterly engrossing.

YEAH, I don't think no matter what you say would get me to go near the edge of that ledge. I'm sorry that's the way it is, I don't like heights. I've even tried to tackle it, but it never seems to get any better. I understand, however, if it were a lifeline I would try to attempt to stop your demise. You know that rational kind of energy that just kicks into motion whenever there is something incredibly horrible about to happen. Yeah, well I suppose I would probably get down to my stomach and try crawling to the edge of the sheer drop to pull you back up. Alternatively, I am pretty fearless when it comes to most other things, but not heights.

IT IS great to realize that I finally belong somewhere now, I'll start Monday, no later. Except, I did not garner 10 years' worth of filling material, so you're going to have to have at that yourself.

OKAY, I promise not to mention anything again. Plus, that also goes for the, "*have you got a dream... seize it,*" ideal. I'm not sure why I am putting this here, but I figured since we are talking about pretty much anything, I might as well. My cousin wants to go see that movie Love, Simon. Not sure why she desires to go see it, but I don't want to bail on her so I said I'd go view it. It's supposed to be about some closeted gay kid. Therefore, it's a new experience for me to witness.

With what you said about the screaming to the high heavens, about what happened. May I ask what exactly you are talking about. Sorry if I am parading to close to home for you. It's just, I am interested in getting to know you and since you mentioned that you have a lot of anger and bitterness or well your mom said you did, from what you stated. I am just trying to piece things together to figure out what transpired.

As opposed to having a little brother or sister, I can happily trade my brother with you for an afternoon... or indefinitely. Actually, I'm joking. I love him even though he drives me crazy. I can't imagine a time there wasn't without him invading my privacy or continually following me. It would be sad to think of a world without my brother, even though I could rightly knock him out at times, but that's brotherly love. You love them one moment, and then you're pleading with your mother after knocking out some of his teeth the next. I'd say... they were crooked anyway.

In all honesty, I have never helped my little bro with his homework, sure we talk occasionally about movies and problems, but I have never supported him with his school work. Perhaps I do have a couple of things to learn from you, and that is something I should do. After all, I am the bigger brother, and I have a legacy to live up to, so, thanks for giving me the inspiration to be a slightly better big brother. I'll do that sometime over the weekend. I'll get him off his cellphone for a while and get him out in the backyard to enjoy some fresh air for a change.

You have legitimately made me crack up. I promise I won't tell you if I decided to take to cross-dressing and to have secret intimate conversations with oneself. Except, lookout, I don't want to be cliché. Consequently, I won't murder you in a shower cubicle. I'll make it my utmost best to think of something new and utterly shocking. And no... I have never heard of the movie called Disturbia, but I'll search for it on Netflix tonight, and if not there I'll see can I get it on the iTunes store. I'll let you know if I think it is a carbon copy of Rear Window. Ah, and cool, I didn't know that. That guy must have some seriously dark thoughts if he invented those creations. Though of course, he would be a genius for reviving the face of horror.

AND HEY, ABOUT THE FRIEND THING' it's cool. I think I can understand how it would appear. I guess there are some people who are naturally quiet who would like to be in my position. Being surrounded by people is fun, just as you mentioned, it is a lot of work. You continuously have to be on guard, in the humor all the time and outdo yourself in every interaction. I will agree that sometimes it would be nice to take a breather, sit down for a minute and not to have to live up to someone else's mental image of what my life ought to be like. If we ever meet after these letters, that is if you want. I promise you, you will not just be a kid who turns up at school to do your classwork and then disappears. I don't see how people would not like you, because you seem pretty impressive.

Wow... I just had a thought. Sure, you made the controversial topic more relatable considering it would appear that way. We know nothing more than what other humans have told us to be true. There is nothing but a story from where we have come from. Everything is a miracle, and I suppose the quicker and sooner we realize that we are just here and that's that, then the more content we can be. We are never going to know where we came from or what our purpose is. The fact we are just here is evident in itself. For all, we know, cats and dogs have no more of an understanding of what they are than we do. We know only a little of what they are and what we are? Everything we consider to be true has been born a story, right down to the piece of paper in front of me I am writing on. It all began as an idea to fulfill a need, and that is how we got here. Stories always have I guess, filled in the missing pieces of what we don't know, but wish we knew. For instance, the Kraken in the pirates' age could have easily been as popular as the idea of Moby Dick in its day, and as presumably, God is/was of today's standing. We humans need something to look up to fear, and something to believe. I believe you have stumbled onto something here. There is just us. If there are other signs of life, it's just them.

ANYWAY, you got me to thinking all about my purpose in life and why we are here. Not sure why, but, I oddly like It. Anyhow. I need to be going. If my friends catch me writing this letter after hours; if they come looking for me, they'll think I have lost a sense of mobility.

SEE YOU MONDAY,

FROM,
    Watson.

ENTRY #12

To Watson,

I WAS GONE LONG before school let out on Friday. I guess you could say it is a little weird considering I'm supposed to be the geeky one, and you're assumed to be the jock. Somehow, it's amusing to see the roles reversed. Currently, it's Monday, so I didn't get to read your letter until this morning. Nevertheless, yeah, I've known for a while that the teachers move the mailboxes daily. I presume you could say you know how the notes get transferred so quickly now.

Over the weekend, my family and I went to an old Heritage Museum to do with the old railroad. The experience was delightful, and I must say I didn't think I'd enjoy it thoroughly as much as I did. My dad is into all that kind of stuff. Therefore, I more or less went for his sake. It ended up being a lovely day out with the family and on the way back we got shakes at McDonald's which are my favorite sort of milkshakes; drove home and watched The Avengers.

Thankfully my folks don't drill me about having to get a

summer job. I should inquire at the library to see if they have any openings for volunteers. I could do with getting out of the house for a while during the summertime because not a lot happens when summer break comes. I find that I am locked continuously inside when everyone else is outside enjoying the sunshine. Holiday time should always be about soaking up the sun and lounging in the water. I can't agree with you enough, that's what makes summer unique. Imagine going swimming in the Potomac River in the dead of winter. The moment you'll pull yourself from its treacherous waters you'll freeze like an instantaneous popsicle.

Touché, I reckon we would all love to live in California equally. I wouldn't mind if I either lived in California or Florida. Both of them are pretty warm. If I were to take one over the other, I'd probably take California because they don't experience anything as significant as hurricanes. I never looked at the rain as something special, but now that you actually mention it I think it's pretty cool. I have never been outside in the pouring rain like you see in all those Hollywood movies were the actor tilts their head up to the drenching sky and is showered.

BUMMER; sorry to hear that your weekend has been altered by ensuing practice. I hope to discover in the next letter how your weekend went. Let me know if the basketball practice ran according to plan or if it failed miserably. It sounds like you're hesitant to let someone else take your chance. I would to if I was given the opportunity to shine. Only if you give up on something so close to the finish line. I don't think you were ever destined to fulfill that role. Sticking with it through thick and thin takes guts. I guarantee if the rest of your team recognized how you're feeling about the pressure being placed on you they'd understand. Perhaps asking for help; some pointers is not as far off in the distance as it initially might appear. If they are your friends, they will know the signs surely. Will, they actually mouth you off if you lost by accident?

As far as the condition goes with getting stuck with my cousin, yes. Everywhere I go, I seem to be appointed to the position of a personal babysitter. I can relate to what you said that your mom is forcing you to drag your little brother everywhere with you. If it's not too much to ask; is your brother Jordan attending our school or is he in a different school?

I'm sure your little brother, Jordon, looks up to you. I'd bet he won't open his mouth about anything. I assume there could be some sort of mutual understanding between both of you. I understand that if I had a little brother and he had secrets, I'd recognize the power of the brotherly bond. It would work more or less as an acquaintanceship. If you didn't see me, I didn't see you.

Yikes, I can see why you scratched out the statement about the lifeguard. If it were me writing this letter, I probably would have restarted the note all over again but after all an old strikethrough knows best. Sure... Lifeguards are *"hospitable."*

I haven't gone swimming in a long time where I was actually able to go down a slide with someone else. I spend most of my time in the water doing laps up and down the pool. I surmise you're a little bit more free-spirited when it comes to fun. Personally, I keep my head down and focus primarily on increasing my lengths and my speed. Fun I think ended when I got into swimming more than just a pastime. I can't say however I have hit my head off the floor of the pool. I hope your friend Coren was all right. Plus, I believe everyone hates after they exit a swimming pool. The 10 minutes that you run around trying to get all your personal belongings out of the locker, dried and dressed, I believe is up there with the 7 AM school shower in the dead of winter.

Even though I don't attend sporting events, I heard the first thing Sunday morning that the Tigers had a defeat. I'm sorry to hear about that. Yeah, I should have figured that you'd be turning up for the occasion without being asked. Still, even if they were beaten, they still hold the respect of the locals and the school. I am sure the Tigers will succeed the next time around. Do you think your brother will follow in your footsteps for the team? I'd personally love if I had a little brother or perhaps someday, a son or daughter of my own to follow the path I had once at one point. I don't know there is a tingly feeling that comes from the notion every time I think about it now. It almost makes me feel proud, honored even if something like that ever happened.

IN CONNECTION WITH YOUR JOB; count your lucky stars, I saw the potential... I kid, of course.

I could have had a whale of a time with your coffee, but now since it's all but long gone, I guess I'll never know. Correct you did clarify that I could drink it, but it would be poisoned. Wow, where is the fun in that? I must live to a healthy age in order to solve all the crimes which are striking the city off guard. How is a good cup of Joe going to help me anyway if I'm 6 feet under? Perhaps I do know a way now if you were to become a King; I'd brew a lovely vat of coffee. You may have at it to see what happens. I place a wager on the outcome. Either you'll cough up more blood than anything else and drown in your own blood. Or two: you barf up a kidney that life will not be worth living after witnessing such cruel infidelity.

I vote for the sticky note's neon sign thingy... I require you to come into work on Tuesday morning dressed like those guys from Home Alone, where after Kevin, lets loose a contraption with a load of pillow feathers on the two thugs. However, I am not one of those workaholics who sleep on the job and pretend they are, in fact, working. Except, I should give you a raise effective immediately for looking out for your boss.

I look forward to plenty of free time per calendar month.

Oh, okay, a banshee sounds fantastic then. Theoretically is that all it does; it arrives in the middle of the night and steals men who are begging for it away. Seems like a pretty horrible way to go if you ask me. Again, from what I hear, all Irish people are drunk, so I suppose if you are smashed, being able to say no is not an option. I'll make sure from now on whenever I go to sleep, I'll close my windows. The Maryland Summers should be enough to render me useless by first light, due to the lack of fresh air.

Let's both agree that we'll never speak of yodeling again. My cousin was using my PlayStation during the weekend. Somehow when I logged onto YouTube, there plain as day in my suggestions, was the yodeling Walmart kid. And for the last two days, the blooming kid has been harassing me in the suggestions panel of YouTube. In the off chance, I should've taken you up on your offer to hear you sing. You may never know; you could have had the voice of a choir boy.

Well, there goes my breakfast. I genuinely thought you would've saved me no questions asked. I understand heights may not be your best point, but, hey at least I won't be hanging for long. I guess we'll see which takes longer: the point where you realize that you need to save me or the millisecond I give way from the ledge. I have some hope of surviving considering you just said that you would crawl to the edge of the cliff to save me.

About garnering 10 years worth of filing material, that is why you have a secretary; they are the ones who are thought to keep everything in check and balance. While I'm off gallivanting about the city, you should be at the office placing index cards in the new filing cabinet that we recently purchased using the taxpayer money.

Yes, I heard about the movie and apparently, it's okay. It's not really my thing. However, I reckon it is a new experience, and new encounters are always worthwhile. I hope you enjoyed the film' whatever it is about. Come Monday, don't let some wisecrack slip back my way concerning my statement. The caption on IMDb states that the character is a guy called Simon Spier, and he has a huge secret: he's gay. Sounds like it's going to be a massive deal in the gay community, for anyone who is gay. Or whatever they call it... I have lost count of how many different names they have for every subgroup within the crowd.

Your little brother Jordan sounds like he can be quite a handful. I politely detest. Do you know how that looks on paper? If you don't even want him, then what in God's name thinks I'm going to want the nuisance. I'd say it would be pretty lonely without the constant privacy interruptions. I surmise you'd get used to little things that other people take for granted.

Still, I love your representation of brotherly love. Gave me a giggle sure; surprised you haven't invented a little competition between the two of you to see who can knock out the greater number of teeth within the given year.

I reckon it's nice to be able to say that... Being able to say that you're a big brother. And when you feel like it' you can just approach your little bro, ask him to hang out, kick a ball around for a little bit. I guess not many people would look at it the same way, but siblings are peculiar things. I hope you got to get Jordan off the cell phone or iPad or whatever electronic device he was caught up in. I find that nearly every bonding situation these days take place over one of the following.

You either meet up with friends or family, exchange pleasantries over a social alcoholic drink. Ideally, the other way of going about it is over a lovely meal, or McDonald's quick-fix; of which half the table's attention is drawn to cellphones, where the chit-chat fades into a bland nothingness until nobody is talking, and all consumed by the virtual reality.

I'm wary now. I'll never be the same if I witnessed you reenacting Norman Bates. At least you caught onto the no *cliché* thing; being new is incredible. Yeah, and I hope you got to see the movie Disturbia. Let me know what you thought of it if you actually did get to see it.

GOOD TO KNOW that you won't be one of those kids who just turn up for the sake of it and then disappear after hours. I'll hold you to that, that is if we ever do meet. There is some sense in what you say. The human population acts a lot smarter than we actually are. We believe we have all the answers figured. We are deemed to be the most versatile species there is. Yet I still have problems trying to figure out what I'm eating for lunch on a daily basis.

Reasonably one day we will all but be a story of what once was. Just like Moby Dick, The Kraken, or religion. Humans have a common misconception of complicating things, to further oneself when it is not necessary. Robots are going to outdo us. For once it would be nice if everyone just slowed down, enjoyed the moment that's around them, and understand that not everything has to be a challenge, question or race.

I get what you mean by your friends catching you. In no way do you have to feel obligated to write back to me. If it takes a couple of days for a reply, I'll understand. All I ask is that you don't forget about me.

UNTIL LATER,

FROM,
    Sherlock.

ENTRY #13

To Sherlock,

I NEVER CONSIDERED it that way. I figure you could say it was a little weird on Friday how I was the last one leaving school between the both of us. Usually, I am long gone when the bell goes, except I decided to stay back to see if you had sent me another letter before the weekend. I am happy I did because you did and I answered your letter all before I left school. Funny I suppose, I was in the middle of writing my previous letter when this guy I have never seen before in my life came into my classroom as I wrote the new message. The dude came in to collect the box, and at the time I happened to be busy penning the letter to be bothered. That was until he addressed me quite rudely.

He said, "*you*' they're... the school day has ended. Aren't you going home?"

I didn't know what to do other than stare back at him, pen in hand, and my eyes were downcasting in my head, as I waited for my brain to come up with an explanation. I never assumed that you are required to leave the school building the minute the final bell rang. I was only going to be about ten minutes tops, and that guy got a little annoyed or something.

I said," I'm writing a letter, I'll only be a few minutes."

Then get this, the guy said, "I'm locking up."

So HERE I was sitting attempting to write you a letter in the odd situation. I was going to ask for another couple of minutes. However, I didn't see the use in it. I mean, I probably would have made the man even more grumpy.

The thing is if I wasn't causing trouble then, and if I were in that guy's shoes, I'd probably have said, "I'll go lock the other classrooms and come back so you can finish."

Alternatively, I packed up and left the classroom with my school bag in one hand, and your letter and pen in the other. Sorry again if you thought your note was a little-crumpled. Everything occurred extremely fast. I didn't have a chance to put it away. So, you might ask as I stood out in the corridor I placed the paper against the wall and began to write over. Only this time as I got another sentence or two down on the page. That dude strolled out of the class carrying the mailbox thingy. In the process, I forgot I dropped my bag by my feet, and when I went to chase after him, I almost fell.

I STUMBLED FORWARD, calling out, "wait...! I want to..."

THE MAN TURNED AROUND and well I almost ran into him. I would have been mortified if I had done that. In the long run, I got the man to leave the mailbox with me. Oddly it felt weird to have a whole class worth of people's personal correspondences. The fellow did his rounds as I wrote at a lightning pace to get down my principles on the sheet. By the time he came back, I had just finished. Lucky I must say, I was.

IT's neat that you got to hang out with your dad on the weekend. My dad works too much, and when he is home, he is the type who does BBQs, polices the game on television or does some DIY around the house without interruption. Dad is not one for affection and personal time. Everything to my dad is seen as a profit; measured for its usefulness or purpose. Whenever you do get my dad on the right side, he is an excellent man. I love him with all that said, though it sounds like your dad and my dad are two entirely different people. Family time in our house is more like a trip to the baseball field or an open lawn so that he can force me to practice running about for a football or to see how far I can kick it. It's cool that you have a dad who is into, I suppose, something different than what most other dads are into.

SPEAKING OF MILKSHAKES, McDonald's milkshakes are delicious; only anytime I pass a Johnny Rockets restaurant I can't help but drag whoever is with me along the way to eat and stock up on an average of two milkshakes. I can't help it, that stuff is gorgeous. I love strawberry, is that your favorite? I have never been one for hotdogs, however, anytime I go to a concession stand or Johnny Rockets, people enjoy having themselves a hotdog. I never quite could understand why people love chowing down on a foot long sausage. May I ask where the Heritage Museum is in the city? If it's close enough, one day if I have nothing else to do, I might stop by if I am in the area. Somehow that will be a little funny. Recognizing that I am in the same location as where you would have been.

I HAVE SEEN The Avengers by the way. Finally, something the two of us have seen, and know about. By any chance, do you like Deadpool? I love that movie. Ryan Reynolds is a legend. I've never come across a film with so many innuendos, as I did with Deadpool. Speaking of movies, I saw the film you asked me to look at. Eh... Disturbia, do you remember. Anyway, I thought it was pretty good actually. The whole house arrest, keeping him from going outside the door is probably nightmarish, considering the dude from Transformers is in it. I can't remember his name... sorry. I found some parts amusing but once shit... Eh, you didn't see me swear. Anyway, as soon the... hmm... the ball dropped everything went to Hell in a hand basket. I appreciate it; for you mentioning the film to me, so thank you.

YEAH, California would be lovely. If I were on vacation, either way, I'd still like to go to California. True they get fewer storms and natural disasters. Nevertheless, they do get horrific forest fires in that part of the country. If holiday time were to be spent in the water, I don't believe I'd choose the Potomac River in the middle of winter. Besides, your statement about freezing like an instantaneous popsicle: that gave me a bit of a giggle. As for standing in the rain while it showers over you as you see in every romance film ever. There's a big difference, I suppose with the rain being warm and the rain being cold. I'd love to hear back whether your opinion is still in motion after you stood in a storm shower and experienced the sensation of it in the middle of winter.

Damn straight; if I can maintain my place in the world for long enough, I won't feel replaced in the space of a heartbeat. Yet again, people being irreplaceable is not a status anymore. It's not the 1940s or 50s because they were different times entirely. These days people are like cannon fodder. You line them up; and knock 'em down without any remorse. Then the people who run the HQ departments, replace them with someone else as if you are a clock, a pencil or car. Meaning, if I stay at the top of my game for as long as I can, then there is no need to want to replace me. I reckon I am a little afraid to step down out of the limelight in case I lose it forever. I've worked so hard to get to where I am; it would be scandalous to let it go.

PRACTICE WENT OKAY, I guess you could say. It wasn't the best practice ever. Still, I think things are looking up. I played a little better than I did the previous workouts, so that's inviting. The only thing I'm worried about now is that after my weekend training, I'm walking around with a knee brace on my right leg. Now here is where it gets a bit shitty, I love wearing shorts. Only, wearing a knee brace and pants together is a little irritating. I would so like to take the option of wearing shorts, but I don't believe it's warm enough in the mornings to do that, not until next month anyway. Plus, it makes it hard to wear my team uniform. I'm more anxious about my stupid leg giving out in the middle of that match coming up.

. . .

I BELIEVE the two of us have the same outlook on the situation. If you give up when the going gets tough then apparently, it's not made for you. My dad has the same type of temperament. Giving up is the sure way to becoming a quitter, and if I did back out of the opportunity, I think he would be disappointed in me. One thing I got accustomed to while working on the team is not asking for pointers. I don't know why, but it's not really something I've ever really thought about with the boys. I guess I could give it a try, but in the meantime don't hold me to it. It's cringey even thinking about it, but I surmise if I do need some help, asking is not the least of my worries.

As for my teammates mouthing me off; sure, it's a real thing. I imagine it comes more or less down to the adrenaline of the moment. The last thing I ever want to hear from people I've come to learn about and love is to be scolded by them. The funny thing is nobody at the time goes out and thinks: well hey that player was trying really hard. Instead, they don't take your feelings into account. They just start picking up stones and hurling them your way.

YEAH, babysitting sucks. Jordan goes to Bellevue Middle School Downtown. I think my mom is going to sign him up for enrollment in my school next year. Something about having to rush around to collect both of us at the same time. Therefore, Jordan is going to be moved to my school so that it makes things easier and so that I can kind of watch out for him. I'd like to believe that Jordan has my back, as I do his. If push came to shove, I assume my baby brother would not rat on me unless it was life-threatening.

IYIYI, I can't believe I wrote that. It looked so cringey and embarrassing. When I was penning the letter, I wish I had more time to go back to the start and begin a new note. Only I was a bit pressed for time that day. I figured it wasn't a big thing if I crossed the statement out. Well, now the lifeguard blunder is awkward.

Consequently, an old strikethrough knows best. Lifeguards are hospitable people lol (laughing out loud.) Ah, that's sad to hear dude. You should totally up your game by including waterslides in your repertoire. I don't think free-spirited has anything to do with going down a slide. I believe any single person can do it as long as they want to do it. I don't presume under the pretenses; that you need to be free-spirited and a bit wild just go down a slide. However, you said you work on pool lengths, then I can only imagine you are twice as fast as me in the water. Everybody hates getting out of a swimming pool. So, the fact that you mentioned getting dried and dressed is up there with the 7 AM shower, I have to agree with you, man... They are the worst times of getting wet and having to dry and dress. Yet, beneath it all they are naturally relaxing moments; who would've believed they could equally be annoying.

THE TIGERS WERE ROBBED of a victory. I went to see the game with my mom, dad, and little brother. Even though I don't play for the team anymore, my dad was a little bit upset that they lost, which was weird to see. Even if the team loses yes, they still have that general respect by the locals. Being a sore loser is not the most idealistic point for a team to be. Yet it's good to know that we still have the hearts of many people that even in hard times they are always willing to give us a chance because it's all they have to hope for. I admit, maintaining integrity in all pursuits when they don't go according to plan is an excellent idea. You should always hold a sentiment of hope in your heart.

Do I think my little brother is going to follow in my footsteps? Who can say for now? All I know is the little doofus has more than enough potential to make a decent attempt at the sport. Yet, if Jordan does not have the attentiveness or the heart for the game, then he'll never make it off the ground. I reckon you could say I made it onto the team by showing it in my attitude of unwavering love and compassion for the pastime. I worked so so hard for the opportunity to be able to be placed on the front lines. If that is what Jordan wants, he's going to have to want it like nothing else he's ever craved before. Except, I do see your point in your statement. Having someone else follow in your footsteps is honoring. If my baby brother decides to do that, then I guess I'll be the happiest big brother ever.

Referring to the office work life, what sort of cruel infidelity are we talking about here now. Are we talking about Gotham type of anarchy, The Purge type of deal, or a laid-back blues kind of crime? I will pretend you didn't say you found a way to poison me if I were a king. Kings can have people beheaded for such attempts made on one's life. But I believe your imagery of hocking up a kidney or drowning in your blood is enough to disturb me rightly so that I will stop talking about coffee forever, let alone look at it the same way again.

But yeah, give me that cheddar effective immediately. I did not open up all those hours on your calendar so that you could laze about now without giving me a raise. It's good to be finally recognized for my endearing involvement.

Indeed, it does sound like a horrible way to go.

According to what my father has said a banshee theoretically comes in the wake of the night and steals men away. Good call on keeping your windows closed. You never know when an Irish creature of folklore is walking about on American soil.

AGREED, although I can assure you I have no voice of a choir boy. If it were my PlayStation, I'd delete my search history... Scratch that my account and start from fresh. I don't believe my senses will ever be able to un-hear, or un-see such a thing.

Once I understand how important it is to take a bold approach to save one's life. No questions asked if I find it safe to do so, and I don't put myself in danger, I would try and reach you. Except we all respond differently in times of panic.

I HAVE GOOD NEWS BOSS... The closet has been cleaned out, and I have placed an order for a new filing cabinet and index cards using taxpayer's money. I hope you don't mind, but I also included a nice mahogany desk and iMac, and a new car to the bill to help me get to work in the mornings. I'll mark the purchases down as something else so that the authorities don't know that I actually spent the money on expendable items.

LOVE, Simon was pretty good actually. For the whole duration of the film, I believed I had an idea of who the mystery guy was that was messaging Simon. Then when I found what I was seeing was accurate, the whole film makes an entire 360 move and completely confuses me. The end was super sweet, I suppose, if that is what gay guys are into or... you know... umm... Are in love, I guess. It's hard to explain. However, I felt incredibly warm watching the movie as the final scene in the film took place. It presented a warm sensation that I've never sensed before, and that was different. I think it is a big deal in the gay community.

The term is given to the community, and everybody within it is usually called LGBTQIA+. Behind the singular lettering, each letter represents a different subgroup within the culture as you may know. Every character is assigned explicitly to the gay population. However, the significant proportion of this abbreviation is from this society. I know how weird it looks now considering I know all this. Except after I watched the movie, I decided to go home and look up what the meaning of what the abbreviation exactly is. I can confidently say I learned something new from watching the movie.

YEAH, Jordie is a bit energetic. Only I didn't see how it would look like on paper. It's not that I want to get rid of him, but now that you mention it, it is kind of funny. I don't think I'd have the heart to knock out my little brothers' teeth on purpose anyway. The little things I do take for granted I'm sure I would miss them if Jordan disappeared all of a sudden. Not that I want him to disappear because he does fill in the proportions of my life that I never really knew existed until I started questioning them. That is my representation of brotherly love. Even though you could tear their head off at one point in time, there is nobody else like a brother, who would take some amount of shit and still love you for it. There is that bond stuck between us, and no matter how hard things may get, we will be there for each other if the two of us really needed it. Simple things like asking my brother to play kick about, or play PlayStation is rewarding in its own right. Sometimes you have to compromise, I guess. I don't want to force all my hobbies on Jordan solely. Meeting in the middle is what I try to do on most occasions. If he plays football with me, the next time I'll have a gaming session with him.

Wow, when you put it like that it really does show how closed and shut off, we've become. Depressing really... how we naturally let ourselves decline into this abyss of technology. I can say I am guilty of doing such an action. I have often had friends sitting at a table with me, and I'd be too preoccupied on my phone to care really. It's hard to explain, even if I am paying attention to the conversation, I know my full undivided concentration is not at the moment. Getting back to the basics is always good, but yes, sadly, it does not happen enough.

COMPLICATION IS UNNECESSARILY MADE NECESSARY. Perhaps that is what the earth really needs right now. A reset button. Not in the way as to turn back time to the dawn of civilization, but just to reboot everything to its natural order and to keep everything the way it is. We need fresh perspective's; and considering we're living in a world with too many angles, it's tiring.

Above all, it is the mentality of individuals who believe what we have built is to be used only for self-promotion and indulgence. Imagine how animals must feel. They share our world with us; yet humans get butt hurt when someone is impeding on their civil rights or attacks their country. What would animals really say if we could understand them; after another rainforest has been cut down, a highway has been built on their breeding grounds, or their pack is slaughtered for profit and not for human survival. We are the worst dictators, yet pretend to be noble, when such a thing is not.

ANYWAY, I really need to go now, I'm writing this letter in between classes. I don't want to be late for the next period. God knows I have teachers who would like to cause unnecessary trouble for the sake of making it necessary.

LAST QUESTION I promise before I go... Did you go out of your way to find out The Tigers' game results so that you could talk to me about it? If so that's really cool.

LATER,
    Watson

ENTRY #14

To Watson,

I THINK I know the guy you're speaking of. Does the man appear to be in his 40s at least, have a stud in his right ear, and have grayish-fading black hair? If so, the person you could have run into is the caretaker. I agree the guy is a little bit grumpy, but not all the time. I remember one time the two of us got chatting about the carbonation process. You know that's when naturally carbonated mineral water absorbs carbon dioxide from the soil. It's the compound added to make drinks fizzy. It also works theoretically speaking with stuff like soft drinks. Don't ask me how I got talking to the guy about drinks and soda waters; during a free class one day out of the blue, when I was returning a book to the library. Anyway, the point being the guy was alright and certainly intelligent. Oh, and yeah, take care the next time you are writing, and you forget about your bag being between your legs. Don't want you in the hospital now, do we? I won't be able to communicate with you then.

. . .

EARLIER IN THE MORNING, I was taken out of class and moved to the vice principal's office with two other students I have never met before either. Funny how we both met people we never regarded prior to the run-in. All the way to the vice principal's office, I was terrified that I had done something wrong, and that is why she called me to her workspace. Only I could not figure out why Ms. Byrne wanted two other kids and me.

WHEN I GOT to her office, I never felt so small in my life before. I mean, I just stood there waiting for her to address us as she finished up a phone call. All along myself, and these other two kids stood oddly, not knowing what to do.

There was another boy. Totally preppy, you know. The kind who think they are better than everyone. The kid is always going around school wearing colorful attire. I talked briefly with him while we were waiting to go into the room. Even for a confident guy like him; compared to me, the guy was a little nervous at being asked out of class too.

The other was some red-headed girl, and she was so so pretty. Only the girl didn't talk much. She gave me the most heart-stopping smile and then acted as if she knew why she was there in the first place. All along me and the other boy were on the verge of rattling. When she said her goodbyes to the person on the phone; she beamed at us and started explaining why she pulled us from class.

IN THE MOST straightforward and shortest explanation

possible Ms. Byrne said that we were example students and that she wanted to bring us together to form some sort of society which utilized all threes backgrounds. The girl ended up being a chick called Sofia Applegate, who is apparently talented in arts and crafts. While the boy turned out to be Justin Blake; who likes acting and has received a modest following. I, on the other hand, am a nobody. Only they wanted me to help out considering my knowledge. Supposedly I am the brains behind this little stunt, and they require me to write a segment for the school talent show that is coming up. You know... the one before summer break. They want to include it at the beginning of the show to raise funds for people who have disabilities. With a push, the vice principal also moved on to suggest that she aspires to arrange a meeting on a school pep rally, considering the spirits will be high, and perhaps people will be more generous with their wallets.

I ENDED up agreeing to the idea, and when I left the room, the drama kid started talking to me. The guy wasn't what I was assuming he'd be like. I usually consider most preppy kids snobby. Except Justin wasn't any of that. He asked me if I was looking forward to working with him and Sofia. I said, "*yes.*" I didn't have anything to lie about. I think I am going to enjoy working with them; even if it is slightly outside my comfort zone.

BUMMER, I'm sorry to hear that your dad does not take home life as serious as some others do, or for that matter like my dad. I guess though in a way your dad makes it up to you in a different way. Perhaps he comes to all your games and shouts from the stands to encourage you. However, I'll tell you this... dad does not get a say on what to watch on tv in our house. Mom is the one who polices the remote. Anyone who threatens to change the channel on her when she's watching something she is interested in can be prepared for annihilation. Do not get me started on the junk mom watches. Frankly, my brain can only take so much reality television per week. The amount mother watches is enough to put even the most avid documentary viewers to shame.

SOUNDS a little harsh how you described your father. I think I know what type of person you are talking about. I don't know what to say other than I'm sorry. Only here is where things differ. My dad never plays sports with me; if it is, it may be poorly prevalent. Sometimes I wish dad did some of the things you mentioned in your previous letter. Still, desiring and hoping is not going to change how my father is. Dad is not practical when it comes to sports or doing DIY. In fact, I would desist from ever seeing him put together a prefabricated chair that comes flat packed with a manual. In specific terms, your dad sounds awesome at other things, my dad can, and would not do.

I CAN'T SAY I am a fan of Johnny Rockets. I don't like the general taste of their food. I presume it is one of those things where we all have our preferences. Nevertheless, from the few times, I have eaten there over the years, they do blend a lovely milkshake. Strawberry is lovely, yes, but I prefer Vanilla with Oreos or an Oreo Cheesecake. Mhmm... Now you have me thinking of milkshakes in the middle of the school day. Now that is totally mean lol. (Laughing Out Loud.)

I love hot dogs, however, plenty of mustard and ketchup for me. Though yes, I never quite understood why they made the bun way smaller than the sausage. I suspect it is just one of those things' humans do idiotically. Nothing we can do. Just pray for our survival.

The Heritage Museum is on the outskirts of the suburbs. Closer to the city. It's on that road called Lambert Road, which connects up with a route that I have no idea what the name of it is. I can get the coordinates for you if you wish to know. Just type into google The Great Old Railway Heritage Museum, and it should come up on google.

That's great to hear. Yeah, Deadpool is funny alright. It's not my favorite, but it sure is funny. Nothing else comes to mind with so many innuendos. I have no idea why the movie As Good As It Gets keeps screaming out for attention in the back of my head; currently as I pen this. Still, that movie also is entertaining, but I don't see how it is anything like Deadpool. I often feel bad for Sinead O' Conner. That poor woman is made fun of in a lot of Hollywood movies. First, Ted, then Deadpool. I am only surmising, but I figure there is more than that out there somewhere. Eh... Yep, I recall Disturbia. The movie is pretty intense, alright. It's exciting. Only, I would not want to be stuck in the same situation as Shia LaBeouf, that is his name. The guy from Transformers. Plus, I have no idea what you are talking about. I never saw you swear. Lastly, I never heard of that expression before. Hell, in a handbasket. I got a chuckle out of that.

YES, California is for the summer. I often wonder how people have endured harsh climates for the sake of it. The most logical fact that humans have to go on; for living in the middle of a place like Alaska or the barrens of Russia is for profit.

It's funny what greedy cooperations can offer, and in return, people flock to these small villages that have uninhabitable conditions. The reason why we bother putting ourselves in the middle of these desolate winters is for that fact; money. If cash did not exist, I doubt anybody would be living in the wilderness way up north for the sake of it. You raise a good point. I don't fancy being outside when a downpour happens with rain that is enough to freeze you upon impact.

TIMES HAVE CHANGED, and I hope I am not too late to make a difference. In days like this, we are told by our parents and our teachers. Even the leading innovators and our friends that anything is possible; everything is up for grabs. People don't happen to mention the fact that it is up for grabs. The pedestal you may be standing on is what someone else is grabbing for. The 1950s seemed like a more innovative and innocent age; when people were honest and had heart, but not a whole lot of competition. The population is one contributing factor. We have triple the size of talent than we did have in the 1900s, and that is what differentiates the olden age from today's age.

You were not as expendable because there was a lack of able bodies. The real question is... will we ever stop, or at least slowdown? Who knows, but have people ever heard of a condom? Our world cannot sustain itself much longer. Every living person adds to the world temperature. Imagine what one billion inhabitants raises the world temperature by. Now plus that for every municipal with more than 1 billion, and times it for every thereafter. We can control people, and the pollution we emit, though not sunlight. You need to practically shine these days to make it anywhere in the world. Giving up when the going gets tough is scandalous.

Good to hear that practice went well. Sorry to hear about your leg trouble. I know how that goes, muscles and joints give up. It is a bitch, but it's good to stay in a positive mindset and power through it. I agree it is much too cold for shorts. I don't think next month will be warm enough either. I imagine we'll see when the time comes around. I can picture how wearing a knee brace must feel. I hope the problem goes away as quickly as possible. Don't be anxious, I'm sure it will pass well before your match comes up. It's two weeks, away, right?

Cringy ideas are usually the ones that produce the best results. There is a fine line when sitting back for a moment to evaluate what is acceptable, and when giving up declares you a quitter. We all have those moments of doubt. They shout at us to keep going. They are an excellent incentive. What do I get from all of this conclusion? In the long run, people who finish what they start are always better in my eyes, even if they fail. Rather than ones, who begin; give up or never try.

Well, that sucks if your team gets rowdy if you mess up. I'd be the type of teammate who comforts his friends; and if they fail, I'd pat them on the back and say, "next time... next time you'll get it."

People hardly think of the player when they are watching live football. How hard a particular person is trying. After all, someone with the heart and drive is not what is going to win the game. It's someone who shows results.

I SEE, so does that mean your little brother is going to annoy you in the corridors. From the way you speak about him, I can already find amusing situations that can transpire from this turn of events. Little brother comes to school one morning... makes a mockery of big brother in front of a group of people. Big brother slaps little brother across the back of the head and tells him to get to class in the largest manly voice one can muster.

YEAH, the lifeguard situation still makes me faintly smile from the blunder. But yeah, I didn't say anything about being a free-spirit to be able to go down a slide. I just I can't. I don't want to go much into it, but things are different for me.

Let's both agree to abolish 7 AM showers if we ever got into the political ranks. We will make the time for starting work and school much later. Resulting in the 7 AM shower being done away with for people. I think you spoke the truth there. Who could have guessed that getting wet and then having to dry is equally satisfying and painful all in one experience?

Ahhh Cool. I get what you are talking about. It's the undevoted love and support for your teammates, and also the community's desire that holds the heart to a team. If we all didn't crave the same thing from the club, there would be no family or following. That's what keeps a team together, the passion and trust. In a fan's eyes, there is always the next time, even if they are crushed by defeat.

It is kind of funny to be able to see that you can notice your brother's potential before any coach can. Though, yes, if you have no heart in what it is you are doing. Then you will never make it to the end of it. Quitters are born that way. That's why many people start something and never finish it. People tell them to spread their wings; to have a taste of everything life has to offer. Before you know it, you are forty, with graying hair, and to keep your youth intact, you add every fortnight hair dye to your tired locks to keep the dream alive. Most people get up in the morning, work themselves until they can no longer. Their body gives up, and only then, they are disregarded because they have fulfilled a purpose. For all the hard work you have done in your lifetime. The only thing you can be guaranteed is a box in the ground.

It is quite peculiar when the X generation today are pessimistic toward Millennials. And how the Millennials are cynical to the generation before them. No one is better than either group; frankly, the parents of the baby boomers would have said the same thing as the X Generation when that particular group was children.

Oh, how we love to lay the blame on other people. The sooner everyone understands it is a universal problem, the better. Perhaps then people will stop the biased assumptions when they know nothing when it comes to every person within that generation. Back then, time may have been physically harder; though that does not mean today's age have it tough either. Standards... we have to meet the standards.

OH, most certainly Gotham type of crime. I have a passion for that type of anarchy. The result is scary and mystifying. Okay, I'll keep the coffee deal between us. Now the vivid imagery of having my head chopped has equally disturbed me. It's odd now that the two of us naturally drew the conversation to a dark conclusion. I suppose the two of us have a twisted sense of humor then. Plus, I have sent on the money, all you have to do is sign the liability suit. No need to read the fine print at the bottom. There was a mix up with the printer. I'll never do anything it quotes at the base of the page. I promise I won't freeze you like an instantaneous popsicle. I may or may not have acquired superpowers from ingesting the Mighty Power Of Kratos. I also used my superhuman strength to restock the closet ... I may or may not have used your desk to hold the junk again. Its all well and done until the IRS come knocking on my office door. I'll buy a company car, and mark the expenditure down as staples. You bought creates upon creates of staples.

. . .

Laughing out loud.... The kid is not that bad; he's just a kid singing his heart out. Nevertheless, I laughed. For which I feel terrible about now... so thank you.

I never went to see the movie. I guess it is bigger than I initially realized. People have been talking about the film most of the week, and perhaps I should give in to peer pressure and see what the fuss is all about. Thanks for the abbreviated version. I am happy that you enjoyed the movie. Love is a powerful thing; sometimes, all the answers cannot be answered. It does make people happy and sad to see the closest interpretation of their emotions on television or the silver screen. Is the final scene when he comes out to everybody?

It sounds like you have an excellent bond with your brother. I envy you. I wish I could have something like that. Being an only child is hard. It's good to know you are trying to keep the bond alive, and not doing it using technology all the time. Life has come to that point. We no longer have the patience to even sit in a room with our loved ones to watch a movie, like those days when you'd buy a DVD and sit down as a family. So, in a way, getting back to the basics is, I guess a thing the two of us can agree on.

You are right, though. Humans make things harder than they need to be. The world we live in now is a money pit. Instead, of calling it a society, I vote we call it Money Pit. I care a lot about the environment. Animals are a weakness of mine. You have no idea how good it is that you brought up the point you made. Nobody ever thinks about animals as if they have emotions. Animals are just like us.

They have fear, sadness, and joy. Humans get hurt when someone steps foot on their land; out comes the shotgun. Only if it were a human in another species territory, it is for sport or profit. Funny how we call an animal lashing out at a human a vicious attack. We both know the poor creature will be hunted down for protecting itself. The humans will call it a liability, a danger to human welfare. When you think about it; who was on whose territory first.

YEAH, this letter turned out to be a couple of A4 pages. God, I am so geeky. Is everyone else writing the length the two of us are writing? I am not complaining; I like talking to you. Just saying; our letters are getting substantially longer.

LAST BUT NOT LEAST, about the Tigers games... well to be honest. Yes, I asked around for the results first thing on Monday morning. I figured I'd have something interesting to talk to you about.

I HAVE TWO QUESTIONS... we should start asking each other random subjects... I want to get to know you more.

1. What makes you smile?

2. What makes you angry?

. . .

ANYWAY, I have to get going to the next class... is it just me or does it feel like a Thursday? It's Tuesday all day. But come on, it feels like a Thursday.

UNTIL NEXT TIME,
    Sherlock

ENTRY #15

To Sherlock,

Happy hump day. Sorry, I didn't get to catch up with you yesterday, only I forgot to check the mailbox to see if I had any new additions. However, I did remember to check today. Yesterday was like mad crazy, and I didn't have a minute to get my mind straight. Our science teacher decided to house an in-class experiment which was going accordingly for the most part. But Nathan Brier put something in his test beaker, and a big cloud of white poof blew up. Therefore, for safety precaution, we had to clean up, but thankfully nobody was injured.

Pretty much... The guy you describe in your previous letter sounds incredibly so like the guy I ran into the other day. The caretaker, you say. I can't remember if the man had an earring in his right ear or whether his hair was a fading black. All I can remember is that it was a guy and that he was a little rude. To state the obvious, I cannot recall what I had for breakfast... Oh, wait fruitloops... never mind.

I'M afraid you have lost me with all the science mumbo-jumbo. In case you haven't already guessed it by now I'm not the brightest student in the school. I think I know the basics, but past that all I know is that science is all that fun stuff that makes the world go around. If I had a free moment, and I got talking to someone about anything, I don't believe it would be about naturally carbonated mineral water. Then again, I have not got an inkling as to what the thing is. Do you often go to the library? I presume you would be considering you're a lot smarter than me. Somebody like me doesn't usually go near the library; never mind reading a book. So for future reference, if any poor fool walks up to me and asks about carbonation, I'll hand them a bottle of mineral water. Thanks for the heads up.

AH YEAH, I want to stay healthy too.

FOR A MOMENT there when you said that you were taken out of class yesterday, I thought you said that you had gotten into trouble. And I was like oh snap.... the man himself has done something crazeeey. My mind jumped to all the scenarios that you could have got in trouble for. If I were ever taken out of class, it would probably because I am in trouble. Ms. Byrne is a pretty likable teacher.

I would have no objections to seeing her go on to become the principal of the school, but I suppose then she would have to reign in her sails and stop being cool. Yeah, I guess it is a little funny. I meet hundreds of people every day, so I reckon it's not really that much of a big deal to me. I mean, if you find it funny then I guess that's neat too. Once you get to my level of popularity you kind of wish people didn't approach you so freely and frequently. Yet still, free classes are free classes.

I WONDER what sort of society you guys are going to make. I am happy to hear that you have been asked to create a new club of sorts for the school. Sometimes when all you hear about is football or Lacrosse or basketball; an escape is nicely appreciated to recharge the batteries.

I can't say I've never felt small, but just sitting in an office waiting to be addressed, I guess, I can say I know what the feeling is like. Only when the two of us experience it, you seem to be moving up the ladder in your academic life, and well I seem to be grilled really hard to perform better at things that I am already trying my utmost best to show.

Not only by my parents; my father, I mean..., but also my team and the coach.

JUSTIN BLAKE, I know him. The two of us occasionally talk when we pass in the hallways in school. That guy is legitimately hard-core into drama. Yes, he has no shortage of friends, but I think that's due to his feminine nature with the girls. Justin is gay, I think, and the majority of his friends are comprised of female companions. Nine times out of 10 whenever I pass him in the hallway, he is chaperoned by this huddlement of girl power. Sometimes this makes him hard to get to and well if you want to catch him on your own for a chat that's twice as hard.

. . .

I GUESS I have nothing to complain about if that guy can't even get a breather. I remember a while back I tried exceptionally hard to befriend him. I remember I watched a shit-ton of Glee just so I could have something to talk to him about. After all, my life revolves around sports, so I absolutely had nothing to talk to Justin about regarding hobbies.

One of the girls from the cheerleading squad came up to me one day and asked if I could approach Justin Blake to put in a good word for my friend to get some of the girls to try out for the squad. Just when I agreed to help, I realize that I had nothing in common with Justin. So, I didn't want to exactly seem like I was begging off of him considering I'd never even talked to him before.

Therefore, regrettably, I spent one weekend watching the entire box set before approaching him. All went well actually: some of the girls that parade around with him joined the cheerleading squad, and well I made a new friend even though he's from a different tribal pleb. As for the artsy girl Sofia I have no clue who she is. Although it sounds from the way, you mentioned everything that you guys are going to bond over the next couple of months really well. I hope you make some new friends, you might need them more than me.

Let me know when you organize the day you guys are going to raise funds, and I'll donate something. Who knows maybe you'll be running the same show on the night of one of my big games. And yeah, I agree Justin is not snobby in any way or form.

. . .

It's okay I've gotten used to it. Actually, my dad doesn't come to any of my games, only my mom. I think I've gotten to the point where I play contently now knowing that mom is in the stands supporting me. I remember a time I worked incredibly hard to get my father to notice me. I once was a child with the stupid notion, that if I tried hard enough, I would be worthy of his time to turn up to watch.

Instead, I got to where I wanted, but still no dad. There is some little part of me deep down wishing that if for one night I could have my father come to watch me play that would mean the world to me. I love Lacrosse, I'd even vouch to give it up if only my dad came to one game; just one game. Then I'd know that just for one time in his eyes I amounted to more than just average.

Your mom sounds pretty awesome. My mom doesn't spend much time watching TV; she mostly reads magazines about home-improvement. At home I don't spend much time on TV; my dad and Jordan fill most of the time policing the remote control. Nothing wrong with documentaries but for me, I find them lame... Blah. My head often feels congested as it is with all the bombardment from social media apps. Any headspace I get is always welcomed. Sometimes I get sick and tired of having to sit through more and more useless shit because in the first place I just want to unwind. Instead, the carefree days of opening up YouTube and playing a song is gone and replaced with an ad at the start, middle, and end of the video. Thank god I share a Spotify account with my brother.

Yeah, I guess. After a while of being second best, I surmise you're kind of left to decide whether you want to hate the one who is loved more than you. I'm no fool, but I can obviously see that Jordan is the more preferable one when it comes to my father. I don't hate my little brother, god no. Except I suppose I have come to despise my dad for picking and choosing. A small part of me wants to hate him, but a little part wants to still hold onto him because after all, he is my dad. Hate is a strong word, and although I can say it so freely here in this letter, the extent to which I feel this emotion is not of what the word lives up to be. I do not hate my dad; I just wish he saw things differently.

WHAT SORT of work does your dad do? Mine is a lawyer.

GROSS, vanilla with Oreos and Oreo cheesecake... what are you thinking? Hershey's chocolate shake is the only shake that should ever matter when going to Johnny Rockets. Their food is so good; I don't know what life would be like without it.

    Yeah, milkshakes rule. Can you imagine a world where the only drink we ever had was milkshakes? I can't imagine how much ice cream I'd be able to eat?

ON THE OTHER HAND, hot dogs are pretty tasty. Filler'er up with everything, please. I know, right... whose marvelous idea was it to design a hot dog bun that's twice as small as the actual hotdog? Sometimes I often wonder that too. How have we survived so long when a lot of us do stupid and crazy crap?

. . .

WELL, you are proficient with directions. Thank you very much. You do realize that the street is like fifteen or twenty blocks.

I'll Google it at lunchtime, so I can see where it is you're talking about. Maybe by the time you read this letter, I will have visited The Old Railway Museum, and we will have something new to talk about.

IT's okay you don't have to get the coordinates, but if you want to you can, it's up to you.

INNUENDOES ARE a thing now in superhero movies. I suppose as a guy who likes movies will you ever get tired of watching superhero flicks. It seems of late that everything being released in Hollywood is some form of an adventure movie with some guy or girl running around with superpowers.

It's everywhere, it's like, it's on Netflix and in comic books now. For a moment I thought we would've been over all this showcasing. Though since most distribution companies are making more money from carrying on some of these long drawn out franchises, I'm starting to lose interest.

Even TV shows are taking a jump back to the 1980s. Everything is riding the wave of the 80s vibe because it is popular at the moment. I wonder when this phase will pass on.

ISN'T the film As Good As It Gets about a guy who has extreme phobias of germs? I can't remember if I saw the movie. Again, I don't know who Sinead O'Connor is, I'll have to Google that at lunchtime too.

From recollection, however, I do remember laughing at the joke when I heard it in Ted. Now when I think about it, I'm not sure what I was laughing about.

Yes, Shia LaBeouf is the name of the actor who played the guy in Transformers.

Do you remember the time he was in a video shouting at a camera, "*just do it*." No idea why that surfaced but, hey, it did.

Sure, money is at the forefront of all our endeavors when it comes to exploration. Only at the same time, I don't believe the currency is the root of why we explore. You can say greed is one, but again that would tie in with money. Folks, I guess just like having something to talk about. Curiosity always gets the better of us, and I suppose a tiny part of us still wants to know what's over the other side of that hill. People are determined to recognize what can be achieved by venturing over a ridge or mountain if we can climb over it.

Knowing what motivates us to explore and venture out is not so much to do with money at the forefront, I believe. I think it's the competitiveness of our race. Everybody wants to be the first human to set foot in the new area that has never been uncovered before. Nobody ventures out for the sake of making money at first. We set out to explore, and if we come across something worth exploiting, then I guess that's how money works. All in all, we set out to do good, but at the same time, do the worst.

GOD, I'm turning into you. I am getting all poetic and shit here that I can't recognize my own writing anymore because it's definitely not something I'm accustomed to writing. Before we started talking, I never used big fancy words like I am now.

I don't even know where I am dragging the sentences from. It's like they are coming from the very back proportion of my head. It's like I know they've always been there, but I didn't realize at the same time.

Alaska is pretty beautiful regardless of whether your there extracting oil or ore. If anything, I think Alaska is possibly one of the most beautiful places in the United States of America. It seems untouched and lays barren to most human inhabitancy.

Occasionally dad used to watch westerns with me when I was younger before everything started to get a lot more competitive between him and me. I remember seeing these cool vast deserts of snow and sand; for some reason, I always found a liking to that sort of society. Everything seemed untouched. Maybe you're right... anything humans put their hand to, they destroy it.

YEAH, Hell in a handbasket is a reference to not being able to escape Hell because the current path you lead in life is bound to end up there. I remember hearing it somewhere, I can't remember where though. However, I googled the phrase, and it seems to be connected with slavery or something, so I'm not sure if I should be using that phrase anymore.

THE PHRASE now seems commendable regarding your statement about how the world is overpopulated. Most people don't plan for tomorrow, and if something terrible were to happen, they'd depend on the government to keep everything operating, and that things hopefully will return to a natural order somehow. Most things that killed humans off to prevent overpopulation or any other adverse have been eradicated, and something as simple as the common cold does not seem as life-threatening as it first was.

Perhaps all these little things that we've tried so hard to get rid of in a way we're helping us in an effort that we never got this far in development. I guess we're overdue for an epidemic of sorts. The more people there are on our planet the more strain it places on not only the governments and our natural resources, but given machines are taking over the natural order, we're going to be overpopulated, over-educated and unable to provide within a reasonable balance to maintain a reasonable day-to-day life.

I KNOW what you're talking about when it comes to being told that you have the world at your feet and that you can do anything you want. The only thing people forget to mention is that you have to sell your soul, lose originality, and equate yourself to rape in certain situations to better yourself. Everything has reached a level of a standard; if you do not fit, you must adjust. If you do not try; you're left for the pits. Everything that we have built or the hierarchy... I think that's the name of what they call the different levels in a corporation or government body. The higher you are up on that pedestal, the more likely you are to have that stool ripped out from beneath you. All we know how to do is compete. Companies like competition because they separate the strong from the weak.

Just like how America and most of the developed world has allowed experienced workers to settle in their countries. Yet people who are uneducated, and have minimal work experience beneath their belt because they do not possess a piece of paper are left out to pasture. When with experience, the person who has the least amount of paper has more experience than the person who holds a piece of paper. So is the question you're really asking when will the next epidemic arrive, who knows considering we have nearly annihilated every single natural impunity which regulates who is strong and who is weak. Instead, we have replaced it with a common courtesy in the form of a pill, which will take all the pain and all matter of sickness. We live in a world now where we no longer know who is weak and who is strong. Most people see an exterior presence when they look at a person, and they think just because that person often seems on an approach that the person is inherently soft. Which most can say is probably true. Who knows who would survive an epidemic because after all our bodies have been susceptible to all the drugs and pills, we have been given for so long, that our bodies have grown accustomed to such devices.

Yeah, the knee is looking up. However, I started to notice that anytime I seem to be walking it clicks. I can feel the bone rubbing against my kneecap anytime I'm standing for long periods or either having to get up or down. Not sure which bone it is whether it's my femur or tibia. My mom booked an appointment with the local doctor to have it checked out to make sure everything is okay with it. I'm sure it's my kneecap. It will be a pity if I have to sit out one of the games due to my knees feeling iffy. Except, it's not the first time I have played with a brace. It's not that hard to play a game with one, but sometimes I feel like I'm trudging on the field rather than running. Sometimes I wish Lacrosse or Football were that easy, but unfortunately, nobody really has that can-do attitude for, "*next time.*"

THAT IS true people hardly think of the player when football is being conducted. Everybody wants there favorite team to win, and when they fail that mission, people often criticize the players who didn't perform to their expectations. I know how that feels. It's like I know sometimes I underperform, and it's not something I like doing, but often or not you give it all you have until you can't anymore, and you just need to pull back. Otherwise, you'll seriously hurt yourself if you don't.

Except, when you do get times that everything is going accordingly, you just feel weightless. I don't know how to describe it, but it's like this fire that rages inside, and all I can do is keep running. I get this breathless sensation, a tingling that's charring inside and all at the same time there's like this static soaring through my veins, and all I want to do is make everybody happy. I know that if I make everybody happy, I'll be happier. Passion is funny. At the same time, love only derives from making others happy by pushing myself to the limits.

Manly voice... more like squeaky. It's like my voice has gotten substantially higher over the last couple of months, and it sounds weird to me that I no longer even recognize it anymore. I wonder when my voice will drop, and it will sound more normal. As for my brother well let's just say I don't think he would be going to class. He'd be getting a first-class trip to the toilet... swirly's are brilliant. If I can get rid of my problem, I'll flush it.

Subconsciously rolls eyes... Don't remind me; my grandmother always said that. Not anymore though she's dead; still, it is annoying when the previous generation points out all the flaws that we have. Like they don't have any to contend with. You don't see us going around, pointing out how we think their generation is lazy and lacks respect. I could speak about them... they can hardly move... and they call us lazy... I know, I know. That was a pun, I know with age you lose mobility.

THE HEART of any team is in the possibility of winning. It will always be that way for everyone. That is why people get rowdy when we don't win. It may be hard for fans to see their favorite team lose. However, for the players who put all on the line throughout a game, it feels like getting smacked by a bus. If that's what getting hit by a bus would feel like. I mean, you know. How pointless and gutted you feel after playing so hard.

I'd know considering I taught him everything the little dude knows. Sometimes people may have the necessary skill for such a hobby but lack the heart. Some may say what's the point of not expanding on that forefront if you have a natural talent. In a way, I guess it does seem like a pretty reasonable argument except what's the point of doing something that you don't have the heart in. Anyways our time on this planet is limited so why deprive yourself of something less when you'd want something more. For many people, they don't understand that we only have one chance to do what is right for us, and many people miss this and settle for less. Rather than starting a bit of everything focus solely on one thing that you could see yourself doing for life, but don't be afraid to of course to dabble in other experiences. Don't commit your life to it if it's not what you're passionate about. All I know is that throughout my life, I want to be able to live it with purpose. If I get to live it accordingly, then I guess that is all I need to feel complete.

I'd love to pursue Lacrosse as a career opportunity, but sometimes I know that that is not the best route to take. I've never told anybody this but... please don't judge. I like classical music and well if I were ever given a chance to become a musician, then I'd like that very much, even as much as I love sports. I don't like to tell people that I like that sort of music because it's not what everybody else is listening to and well... I just want to fit in. Yet when I listen to this music, it's like everything that I have ever believed or understood makes logical sense. As I listen to the melody's it takes me away, I can see myself doing nothing other than wanting to create such pieces to inspire other people who maybe like me.

THAT GOT DEEP ALL of a sudden... huh. Anyway, Gotham city... Yeap anarchy is pretty much the only crime that authority ever listen to. When the police force risks losing control, that's when they all panic. Do you like scary and mystifying? I'm assuming you like Halloween then. Halloween is pretty cool... I like it. Whom am I kidding, I love it. At Halloween, you can be whoever you want to be. I guess the two of us have the same twisted sense of humor.

I do like some dark amusement, but when stuff gets overly grotesque, I don't prefer it. I'll just take your word for it that there is nothing of a sinister nature at the bottom of the page and I'll sign away my life probably. Let us hope that the next ice age does not arrive earlier than expected. Otherwise, I will be an instantaneous Popsicle. Plus, that is not fair. I worked incredibly hard, moving all that junk from my desk.

Therefore, I have placed all the lovely belongings out on the curbside and labeled them free for collection. So, we might have a damages suit coming our away in a couple of days for violating clients privacy rights.

Yeah, the movie was pretty big in the gay community. You should definitely see it because it's a surprisingly good movie. So watch it.

DON'T BE SALTY... being envious does not make it all better. I should know I've been jealous long enough and it has no advancements only repercussions. From the sounds of it, everything in your life is pretty awesome, and for once in my life, I wish I could just say freely that I'm smart and that my dad has time for me. My brother is the favored one; I still love him regardless. I've often wondered what it is like to be an only child. I bet you get everything you've ever want and have parents who are so proud of you. That is why sometimes I try to remind myself that it is not Jordan's fault; it's my doubts. I don't want something that miniature in scope to come between my little brother and me because of my father's incompetence.

AMEN, the days of sitting down and watching a DVD are over. I remember when we were younger, we used to go to the Blockbuster stores and pick out movies to watch and load up on snacks, drive home, and spend the entire Friday evening watching family movies.

Ah... yeah, humans have a natural habit of that. Making things harder is the sure way of weeding out the brainless ones in the pool. I'll second that vote for calling the world a money pit. True... Nobody ever thinks about animals as if they have feelings. Like any time, my mom and dad get into a bit of an argument, or when me and my brother fight, our dog Sadie goes running under tables and chairs. So, for what it's worth even though we can't always understand them. Dogs, cats, even cows, and pigs feel just how we do even if they can't talk. Humans still want to be the dominant animal, so, that's why we make rash decisions.

ANYWAY, I think this letter has turned into a pretty lengthy letter I must say. If you think you are geeky, then I'm not sure what I'm supposed to be. And no offense taken, I like talking to you too. It's kind of cool how our letters are getting a lot longer. I remember talking to one of my friends today. I had asked how many pages they were writing to their penpal, and well he said a couple of lines. Therefore, I think we're in the lead, that is until I find somebody else who can outdo us.

THANKS FOR GOING out of your way to find out the results of the Tigers game. It's pretty neat that you did that. I've really grown to like you as a friend; even though I've no idea you who you are. Except, I hope maybe one day the two of us can meet and carry on this friendship that we're building here because you seem real... unlike most people.

. . .

LASTLY, I agree we should ask more questions to find out more things about each other.

Q1. What makes me smile?

A1. To be honest, my music. I feel like I make a difference whenever I'm playing the piano. I smile when I hear goose-bump' worthy music rushing from my speakers in my bedroom. Music makes me smile. I can't imagine my life without it, it's kept me normal.

Q2. What makes me angry?

A2. Not being able to say something that's on my mind. I'm told a lot that I should keep my mouth shut because it's best for everyone and well... Sometimes I just want to voice why I am upset. Sometimes my dad does spend time with me, but not in a bonding sort of way. When we go practicing for Lacrosse or football, he is always grilling me or pushing me.

    It's always... "*focus Max.... or stop playing around and practice.*"

YIKES... Ignore that scribble. It's my name, and I forgot we're not supposed to do names here... Well not until a later point, I think. Anyway, I should really get to lunch now. I spent the majority of class writing this letter.

· · ·

WHAT ABOUT YOU?

OH, and my questions are,

1. What is your favorite band or singer?
2. What is your favorite childhood memory?

WELL, I should be going, I hope this letter isn't too corny.

LATER,
    Watson

ENTRY #16

To Watson,

No worries were all cool. I didn't have time to reply back to you yesterday either. I had to leave school early for a dentist appointment. I know, of all the things I had to leave school for, I had to go for that. Candy is like an omen and a gift all wrapped up in one. I know I shouldn't be eating that amount of sugar necessary on a daily basis, but how can you not, that stuff is addictive. I guess you can say that the best time to catch me if you wish for me to read any letters you write would be first thing in the morning. Therefore, if you leave a note for me the previous evening, I'll receive it the following morning at registration.

Yikes sounds like you had a crazy day. The name Nathan Briar sounds familiar, but I can't seem to construct a face in my mind to who you're talking about. Thankfully the little safety precaution worked, and the school did not need to be evacuated. I heard nothing about a science beaker exploding. What were you guys even conducting to cause such a chemical reaction? You know what, perhaps, I'll just leave that part to the imagination... then I'll really get the memo of how utterly clueless you might be when it comes to what chemicals you should and should not mix together according to the table of elements.

IT'S ALL RIGHT, don't sweat it. To be honest, I don't think I'd have paid much attention either for the fact that the two of us got talking one afternoon. Though yeah... the guy has failing black hair and a stud of some kind in his ear. You must have a clear mind then... I remember most details, and I guess that is why I have so much in my mind all the goddamn time.

I have been suffering from headaches for a while, and I haven't told my anybody. I spend a lot of time in reflection since it's what I'm good at. Living in your head too much is not healthy, and it causes a lot of inner turmoil that you don't get to see on the outside. Sometimes I get fixated on a particular problem that I can't understand and sometimes I don't give myself the proper pep talk to try and calm myself down or take a step back. I keep going and going until I have these massive head-splitting migraines to the point that light hurts.

SCIENCE IS my escape since I don't do anything else... yet at the same time, I am also trapped by my hobby. The world doesn't exist outside those bounds, and anytime I go to try and take a breather all I can think about is what my passion is saying, even if it is slowly driving me over the brink. I guess what you have to come to realize is that science is all mumbo-jumbo. You're doing just fine, so don't put yourself down just yet. I think with anything you take on, patience always gets you through the day. Plus, I believe it when you say that if you are ever to get talking to someone, it would not be of carbonated water. I know how this must sound coming from somebody like me... I probably seem really ridiculous, but oddly it captivates me in a way that normal capacity conversations don't account for. Sometimes I often feel a little offended that someone would waste my time talking about the weather when there are more important things to talk about. Like what gets you up out of bed in the morning. Or, how do you think a game of Dungeons & Dragons will end? Except don't do what you will with the information I have provided. If you do happen to run into a poor fool who is talking about carbonated water, it probably will be me... so don't make fun.

How bad do you think I really am? I said I am pretty much a Brainiac... I don't go around deliberately trying to get in trouble because it's fun to do. Moreover, I don't believe I would be getting in trouble for something considered mundane. If I were to ever get in a dispute, I will assume the reason for being would be more science related. I'd probably rig the door of a teacher's car with explosive diarrhea; that when he or she pulls the handle of their car, a boom goes off inside the compartment and smears the windows brown.

If I may ask what scenario or should I say plots did your mind concoct about me when you believed for a moment that I was in trouble? I have never been in trouble in my entire life. I guess you can say I've been the goody-goody shoes' type of student. I have always been on time to an appointment and for school... I've never contributed to misconduct or truancy or anything else that you can possibly imagine in my educational life. When I'm at home, I'm quite centered and friendly. I presume you could say exceptionally quiet. That's me. I just make a small carbon footprint, and nobody notices me. In a way, I admire being able to be that way. Just sometimes I wish I had someone new to talk to: you know other than my lab partner in science.

Ms. Byrne is a pretty good teacher, but I don't think she has it in her to become an actual principal. She lacks the finesse that the school may need, and I coherently believe that if this establishment were in demand of a new director, I think one would be brought in, with no disrespect to the vice principal. However, your depiction about how she might reign her sails in is quite an observation. Most people don't think of it when they see a teacher or principal. Most just see what they represent on the outside, and I guarantee they were fun... some still are. Yet with time and climbing the corporate ladder, sometimes you have to act more mature than you really care to admit. Being a director of a school is quite a responsibility. Just one person has to cater for hundreds of possibly thousands of students and faculty. I'd love to be able to wager the prospect that people who are in the principal's office were once carefree, but as time went on, they reserved themselves for something more important. It's funny how people will say that you're climbing the ladder in life and that you are reaching new heights when realistically you're losing a part of yourself to subconsciously better yourself... now ain't that ironic.

. . .

I have not got a clue as to what I'm supposed to do for the new club. We never really spoke about what sort of roles we should undertake or outline a mission to achieve. However, it is still early days in the development, and I am confident that things will go well once we get the ball rolling. I'm not sure how I feel working with other people. On the contrary, I prefer to work alone. I'm honored to be given the opportunity, I can't say what the odd sensation feels like when I ponder the moment. In a sense I seem proud yet in the other I'm a little scared because it's uncharted territory for me.

Is that your way of telling me that you know what it is like to sit in the reception area waiting for the principal to call. Are you what girls call, "*a bad boy*."

As a matter of fact, the meeting with the vice principal the other day was my first time in her office. I could have sworn I was rattling when I was heading on inside. The way you talk about being mistreated sounds like you're quite sad about it. Have you ever told anybody else that you trust, about how you feel? What about your mom... she sounds dependable and courteous. If you feel undervalued; just know that what the two of us have here right now is valued. I know it's nothing much considering our circumstances, but I just want you to know that you seem like an awesome guy. So, I can't see why not as to mention it.

SURELY IF YOU were to go to someone who'd listen; they'd probably give you better advice than I could. If you want, I can go to the counselor in school and ask for guidance. Perhaps what I would be able to learn from her, I might be able to help you with. That is of course if you want me to do this, I don't want to betray your trust. I don't want to go and tell anybody about your emotions and beliefs to anybody else without your say-so. Possibly you could have a discussion on peer pressure amongst your team, and say that you are supporting a change, as a hint. I really don't know what to be saying here, but I'll try to find some more answers, and I'll get back to you.

Oh, right, cool. When I recollect Justin Blake, now, my cognitive memory remembers his face about the school building. I never really take much interest in what other people do with their time, but now that you mention it is rather peculiar since I recognize some traits that Justin showcases. I thought the kid is a little feminine. Except, I never attached my conclusions to anything other than that. Now everything is coming into place; drama... a mob of girls... and well if he likes Glee, well... do I really need to state the obvious? I have heard about Glee, but I've never watched it so kudos to you.

Doing the same thing day in day out regularly wears you down. Even if sports is a great pastime for you, I am assuming after a while there are times that you like to step away and clear your mind. As much as I love science, I can't help but having to step away occasionally to refresh my perspective before rushing into something new. A lot of times, people tend to rush into judgments before weighing the pros and cons of an idea. I'm speaking both from experience and inexperience here... There have been times when I have rushed into an uneducated decision, and then the annoyance thereafter, of having to deal with my mistake, is incredibly felt. Sometimes the simple things are often overlooked like taking a rest when you most desperately need it.

. . .

I'm glad to see that your idea worked after all. I have never watched Glee, and I don't believe I ever will; it's not my sort of TV series remember. I like anarchy and stuff like Gotham. It's rather generous that you went to the extreme to learn something about the other person before approaching them. I reckon it makes your proposition softer than coming in gruff and to the point from the start.

As you know, I tend to keep to myself, so I don't make many friends outside my homegroup. If it is, it is usually for complicated matters, I assure you, or I am being forced to commit to the act. However, I think I am going to enjoy working with these other people. Since I started talking to you, you have expanded my horizon in a way. It's like when I wake up in the mornings now, I want to do something new with my time and meet new people. Typically, in the mornings, I crawl out of bed and force myself to the breakfast table, then school.

Except, conversing with you has changed my temperament. I have never bothered to make friends, I like my own company more than people. Now I see I was wrong... There are quirks and good possibilities for interacting with the folks around you rather than shutting yourself off completely. Therefore, I thank you for expanding my confidence.

I WILL LET you know when everything goes ahead, and if I hear about what we are supposed to do, I'll also clue you in on that.

SORRY TO HEAR that your dad doesn't make enough time for

you. Do you feel disappointed when he doesn't show up to any of your games? Do you think you'd play better if he turned up to just one game? I figure I have an idea what you're talking about when you say- you try exceptionally hard and see no reward, and that becomes disheartening. The way you mentioned that you got to the highest position on the team that most boys would love to be in that place. Whereas, you don't feel any attachment to the role and you would rather your father turned up for a game. Sometimes I often find that people are oblivious to how they treat people. Often or not, you may have to voice the reasons to the individual for them to realize that they have a cause and effect from their actions.

I'll leave you something my mom always says to me... "Don't let *anyone* prevent you from doing what makes you happy."

The Lacrosse is your *happiness*, therefore why should you give it up for anybody: even if your father is the one being the inferior one. Don't belittle your dream because sometimes, all we have is our dream. Sometimes we believe with the one-time idea that if we work hard enough; that's where we'll be in an X amount of time, with Y being the goal.

Perhaps I'm not phrasing it correctly, but what I really mean is that the defining moment, everything is rather pointless. Sure, we have pockets of happiness, but nothing ever comes close to achieving something you're proud of... people may be pleased with what you have accomplished personally, but when you want something that could not possibly happen, then you have to prepare yourself for going on without it.

. . .

It's rather funny to hear how our families are complete polar opposites. Yet, the two of us seem to be getting along swimmingly. My mother would never pick up a book, let alone a magazine. On the other hand, my father reads a little bit, but not the same ability as to what your mother probably would read a magazine.

My dad believes television decays brain cells and usually controls how many hours the family consumes content on it. In some way, I have to agree with my dad... It does not vaporize your brain cells like the statement suggests it does.

Instead, I think the whole problem revolves around the distraction and how you can become consumed by it.

Dad is always on my case about spending two hours an evening using video games or TV. In a way, I'm thankful I get to experience a whole handful of other hobbies that lays to waste. Why would you want to be constantly sitting in front of the TV screen when you could be creating art or writing equations for the distance between two stars.

A good book gets the imagination pumping better than any TV series could possibly offer. I think in the last 25 years people have substantially gotten lazier and have resorted to the more natural options of consuming entertainment. Perhaps that is why your head feels compact all the time. Learn to get away from technology for a while. I know, right... Spotify and music all day are life goals.

It's good that you don't view your brother Jordan negatively. Nothing good will become of it. Plus, either way, it's not his fault. I am assuming the way you talk about your brother, then Jordan has no grasp on the situation between you and your father.

Sometimes being the preferred one can often be a hard position to be placed in. I have seen it happen before. My mother is one of them. Her father prefers my mothers' sister Isabel over my mom, and even the stigma has been rubbed off on the grandchildren. It's like just because we're not my aunt's kids we are treated slightly different when you go visit our grandparents.

I don't think it is intended, but it does have effects on families, so I know. Staying in that temperament, however, and trying not to act out on it is a harder task. I hope nothing comes between you and your brother because family is all we sometimes have. When you hold the least bit of fate, they end up being the only people to have your back. If they don't; then what's the point of having trusted individuals.

I suspect from what you stated with your words, is that you are just envious... that particular emotion passes like the rain. I hope you don't change your mind at a later date and decide to seek out redemption for the favoritism going on. There is already enough hate in the world, so the way I look at it is, why add more.

As for what job my father has; he is a computer technician. I figure it's not as cool as being a lawyer where you can tell people what to do... yeah... I rushed into that statement and didn't think of the repercussions. Sorry.

Moving on, how could you mention such a scandalous thing. Vanilla Oreo's and cheesecake are mouthwateringly brilliant. In terms of what I am thinking, well... Hershey's chocolate is ewe. I like the finer things in life like... Oreos because life is not complete without Oreos.

So are you saying that Johnny Rockets is better than your own mother's cooking? I have to say I prefer my mom's food than I do Johnny Rockets?

Mom's cooking is like no other and life without it well... I don't know what life would be like without it. Perhaps I should get my mom to buy more ice cream occasionally. I could make a right milkshake maker out of her yet.

I wouldn't disagree with the milkshake idea and having a continuous consumption rate. Can you imagine rainy days... Netflix, ice-cream, and a comforter... that's all you need. Except it would have to be Oreos every day for me and no Hershey's crap.

Perhaps with hotdogs, we could create a smaller bun so the people will finally get the memo the hot dog exteriors are too small for the actual hot dog. Proud inventors aye...

YEAH, my active pursuit has never been with directions. After all, you're a natural pioneer, so I'll leave it to you to figure out the exact location of the historic building. Do I bother giving you the coordinates instead? I'm assuming you googled it by now and well... you'll have the directions.

This is going to be hilarious; I can't escape my father's voluptuous talk regarding old steam-powered trains, but now I get to regurgitate it from a fellow peer... I'm drowning in joy. I'm kidding, of course... for you, I will happily parrot and listen.

OH YEAH, superhero movies are full of innuendos, and that's

why people in Hollywood love them. Are you kidding... I'd never get tired of watching some dumb ass get kicked around on the silver screen. Of course, superheroes make great money, so they are going to milk it for all it's worth. Only people like adventure and mystery... that's why a lot of superhero movies do well.

According to the polls, fighting superheroes are going to be around a lot longer than us. Nonetheless, the trend we are riding right now, I don't think it's going to end anytime soon. Marvel and a lot of other studios have big expectations.

80s vibe... are you talking about everything that Netflix is pumping out? I have to say I rather like the 80's so they can keep that vibe going for a while.

Yes and no. As Good As It Gets is a film about a guy called Melvin Udall who has a phobia of germs, but it's more of a comedy about him overcoming the rational fear, and trying to become more of a people person. The film is hilarious, and I love it because it's my sort of sarcasm that emulates throughout the entire production.

Yeah, why do we do that sometimes... I guess when people are naturally laughing, we want to be the last one to be chuckling. So, we kind of fake laugh in order to pretend we are enjoying the joke... when in reality, we have no clue as to what it all meant. It's been a long time since I was on YouTube, but I do remember a guy shouting at the camera, "*just do it*."

I never really paid much attention to it... though yes, I do recall people making memes out of it, and that was amusing, I guess for a while, but then again, I lost interest. There's something new about me that you probably don't know.

I have a short attention span, and if it doesn't fit into one of the boxes I'm interested in, I lose interest within a couple of hours.

WE EXPLORE to see what we can, of course, gain from our troubles. You're right that not every endeavor is to profit, but when profit is at the marginalization of the idea, then everything is based on the presumptuous currency that can be made.

Talking is what starts the adventure and of course, with telling you also evaluate how you can make money. Everybody has needs and wants and aspirations and of course, if you can figure out a way to jumpstart in front of them before they have the chance to achieve it, then you will profit from it.

As with your reference to a hill if you are eager to gain money from the knowledge you know; then no mountain is to steep for you to climb. Sometimes it's the intuition we conceive. Not a lot of times: do we follow the voice in our head that tells us, "*what if* "... what if we could do this. A lot of people ignore that voice and settle for mediocrity... When you follow that voice that says *what if...* that's when the best interests of humans come to life.

MORE TIMES THAN NOT, when people are given an incentive to explore when they are not driven, then you usually are motivated. Folks who are encouraged, but don't reach a level of fame they expect to, are indeed the ones who are talented. Everyone wants to be the first to do the beginning of everything... except there is a lot of competition out there. It brings us back to the point we made about the 1950s; how there were fewer people to compete with. Now everybody's skills are almost accustomed to each other that the sense of individuality and richness have dwindled to the point that nothing is no longer valued because the novelty value has already been set way below par before someone has even begun. Or just perhaps, the world was to busy killing to really care.

From the sounds of it I guess you are turning into a mini-me; all poetic and shit... you did not hear me cuss by the way. I reckon I am on my way to the path of treachery from talking to you. I'm kidding of course, but I'm just saying, I would have never dared use profanity so freely. It seems oddly satisfying in a way I never knew would be possible. I think I may grasp how you feel now; how you felt when you made the first advancements in using fancy words. The words just formulate and poof you have a new Sherlock.

ALASKA IS GORGEOUS. The ruggedness, the trees, the wetness, the greenery... or what of it that exists; let's not forget about the snow. I have never been to Alaska, but maybe someday, I hope to get the chance to travel when I leave school, and that is one place I'd love to see.

If you're interested, I can book you down for a ticket already? I'll need a travel partner; as they say, exploring the world on your own is fun and all. However, traveling it with fellow enthusiast is the way it should be.

I'll take it back... I think you are becoming more of a loner than me by the sounds of it.

YOU DEFINITELY ARE GETTING all poetic and shit. "Barren!... Lays barren to human inhabitancy."

. . .

From the way you phrase that statement, it almost insinuates that you have life all figured out... I barely know what I want to do when I leave college, and I'm supposed to be the one that is pretty confident about where I'm heading in my future.

It sounds like your father, and you had some sort of bond when you were younger, and perhaps as time went on, things faded out. Maybe it started to change when your younger brother was born.

Sometimes that happens that the youngest of the family always seems to get the baby treatment; as if they are fragile and you could break them by looking at them. You know what I mean... everyone is on their side and well who is ever on yours?

Maybe you should sit down with your father one evening and say, "hey' want to watch a Western?"

And yes, to answer your question, I have never heard of Hell in a handbasket. Except if it has some bad stigma attached to it, maybe you should refrain from using it. People don't plan for tomorrow because they believe that there is nothing worse that can possibly happen to them. When in truth, everything is waiting to happen.

My grandfather always used to say that people are one step away from poverty, and it's quite frightening when you realize that it is inherently correct. Once you know that no matter what we own is only on loan; you start to evaluate and appreciate things that have no value applied to them. You can always replace the chair, but you can't replace a mother or father, or brother... your dreams.

. . .

YEARS AGO, a deterrent would have controlled the population of the world and of course, weeded out all the weak people who could not stand up against the common cold. I do think we are in store for something radical that will change the world in some years to come, but I don't believe it will be in the form of an epidemic.

I think we will be our own failure more than anything else. I don't think it's going to be some virus. If anything, humans are the virus and will destroy whatever it is we have created because it has been done before in many ancient civilizations.

The population is only set to grow more prominent, and of course, it will put more strain on our global demand for food and of course our natural resources are depleting. What we need right now is a world order that will fix things and try to give earth the chance to give birth to new ideas.

Simpler times called for more hospitable means and being over-educated only makes us cynical and unkind. In the past, we aspired to knowledge as if it were a cure. Yet now what do we aspire to now... I think the random act of kindness is the only thing that gets us through the day, in this day and age.

Like I said before, originality used to trump everything, but now there is no such thing as originality. I think for many years of our lives as we grow up; the way society has been set up, it is a distinctive means to teach humans to behave in a specific manner. In some weird form, not only in our need for knowledge we also give in to the temptation that we may secretly be getting brainwashed.

In a way, it is done so cleverly and so professionally that not even the teachers who are doing it realize they are perfecting it. We sit and regurgitate it on the other end, but do not conceive that we are being brainwashed. From a young age, we are told what to do, what to think, and what to feel. Therefore, when the time comes that we must spread our wings, we are unsure about what we are supposed to do when we have been guided all our life.

For the younger years, we are told to block out the "what if" voice, and just listen to what people of higher-ranking officials will say.

I GUESS we are a little biased in that sense. Every country wants the best populous, and most will want to weed out the weak-minded. Eventually, we will reach a state where we will have too many educated people and not enough to fill in the ordinary gaps.

I'm not being disingenuous here... I don't judge anybody based on their lack of a former education, but we do need people who will still help to support our society we've built. Perhaps in the future, we will no longer need technicians but will need farmers to continue a supply of food. People get so caught up on a piece of paper that they forget what life and experience really is.

How do you really put experience down on a piece of paper... you can't just put anything like that on a piece of paper. We have gotten to the point now that we no longer even look across at our neighbor and say I wish you well... and if you have any problem, don't be afraid to ever knock on our door.

Sure, we give them the friendly impression they are hoping; the rest is up to them and what they make of our impact.

. . .

Good to hear that your knee is a little bit better. Yeah, perhaps you should get your leg checked out to make sure everything is okay. I know a bit regarding bone structure, and well one thing I do know is that athletes do suffer from kneecap disintegration. In a sense, you file down the bones in your knee when you use them more. I hope you don't have to wear a strap for long; it's not nice at this age having to wear a band for support.

Losing the power of your legs is tough, I guess... I guarantee anybody who has would feel pretty worthless, not being able to walk to the store to buy milk. We take such a simple thing for granted. Take better care of yourself, and your body will take care of you. And I can imagine playing Lacrosse with a brace on your knee is going to be pretty uncomfortable.

Hopefully, you won't have to wear one for very long and that everything will be okay before your next big game.

When you feel weightless, or the electricity you describe; that only derives from something you indeed are passionate about.

Keep at it because there is not a lot of times in our life we will experience such a dominant characteristic.

Sometimes we perform best when we have these magical feelings, and when they do present themselves, they can do incredible things.

Okay, you got a chuckle from me... squeaky voice. I guess my voice has gotten squeaky. I think mine has broken, so, I think I am on the path to recovery. I know it's weird, right.

It's like when you talk, sometimes you can no longer recognize who you are or the voice... the little kid voice I'm talking about. It's like one day you wake up, and it's gone... then your speech is all gravelly, then whiny, and then well now my vocals are very low.

I'm assuming that's what will happen to you. I read it in a book before that it happens to everybody, and this seems to be the way it goes. People get it at certain inter-falls within their teenage years. For some, it can happen later in the years, and for some, it can occur earlier. Thankfully, mine occurred just before I came back to school this year. After Christmas the voice kind of disappeared and now I have this low chilled type of voice.

OH YEAH, I get the same lecture occasionally from my grandparents.

If I had a dollar for every time, I heard the statement that our generation is disrespectful or to forward, I'd be a millionaire by now. Except, that burn though...

I would not say that to an old person because... that is what you call a burn. Do you mind if I steal it and add it to my personal favorite sarcastic one-liner diary? I have this random collection of quotes in a small pocketbook.

Sometimes when I'm finding something to say as an offensive maneuver, I like to have a stockpile worth of insults ready. Every so often I rehearse the lines, but I've never actually had to implement them yet so go figure.

THE PLAUSIBILITY of winning for any team is always in the possibility. Everything starts as a possibility, and I guess that is what drives excitement. I can say that is another form of what if. People like to see something that they wish they could do, unfolding in front of their eyes. That's why we have spectators, we hope we can be doing what they're doing, but probably many don't try.

So ARE you taking the glory for your little brother? That if he gets to international fame are you going to come forward saying you self-taught him everything you knew. That's quite risky... What if Jordan makes a dumb move and all the limelight will come to you. I guess there is some point in what you make; some are not fortunate to try their dreams because they may lack the skill, finances, or many other things.

I often wonder how some people get to where they get. It's funny how there are a select few who are given a silver spoon in life; and others who do not. After all, there are many people who have fine skill but no support. You should definitely do something your heart is dedicated to. Why take a vacation if you love something?

If you have to take a vacation every year from doing something that you are not passionate about then maybe the career choice you are living was never for you. You should never let the opposition of money come between you and your passion.

Of course, many people want to be comfortable, and I get that, but you can always have a backup plan. Perhaps safeguard yourself, and then go after your dream.

I won't tell anyone that you like classical. I think it's pretty neat actually. It adds something new to the table that is not usually brought to most people's attention. I don't know anybody else in school here that likes classical music as the way you may do. Most people love music, but many would be quite secretive about saying certain types of music that moved them to tears.

If music is what you're genuinely passionate about and you like Lacrosse, pursue music and play Lacrosse as a pastime. If you could spend the rest of your life doing what it is, you live and die happily fulfilled, then let the music take you away.

I LIKE HALLOWEEN SURE. I don't feel as warmly about it anymore because I don't really do it. I tend to stay in most Halloweens. I remember there was a time I used to go trick-or-treating, and I loved all that, but I don't get to do that anymore.

Plus, I love overly grotesque stuff, so I'm extra twisted. Secondly, I'd like to motion your statement that an instantaneous Popsicle may be coming very shortly.

I AM undecided if I should fire you considering you broke so many civil privacy rights by placing all those boxes out on the curbside; all day my office phone has not stopped ringing since I left work.

I HAVE NEVER HEARD that phrase before, but it's funny... don't be salty. Yeah, I'm sorry it's just sometimes I'd like to be like a normal kid again. Things are different for me. Plus, I'm the only kid in the school that's... Yeah, never mind.

Just I have some reasons to be envious, and I didn't mean it that way okay. I might be knowledgeable, but that doesn't make me smart. Yet there is so much more I wish I could do than just being smart. So don't doubt what you have because when it's gone, you'll never be the same.

I REMEMBER PICKING out DVDs too and watching them every Wednesday and Friday with my parents. Sometimes I wish I could hit some sort of a rewind button to go back to the days when everything was... well... was.

MAYBE WE SHOULD MAKE a how-to book for dummies about how to make everything in life easy. I guarantee it would sell like delicious pastries. And yeah... Nobody talks about animals having feelings. They certainly do have emotions because if a dog is running around with joy to see you then obviously they feel something. Animals can sense things you know because when they get scared, they retreat, of course... when we get fearful, we withdraw too.

I KNOW your last letter turned into a pretty lengthy one, but I think mine has put your previous note to shame. Maybe, for the time being, the two of us can be geeky. Having a companion who is also a weirdo like you is much better than being a lonesome weirdo.

Yeah, I think I have just surpassed the original marker for a lengthily letter already... so your friend has to beat that.

PLUS, don't sweat it. I liked asking around to see how your

team did. You're pretty awesome too, and I wouldn't say no to being friends when this is all over.

I THOUGHT as much that you'd pick music to make you smile. Me personally what makes me smile... seeing people do good. When people reach out unnecessarily, it always makes my heart flutter.

BETWEEN YOU AND I, I will never tell you to shut up... so if you ever have anything on your mind I am willing to listen. Maybe you should ask him to back off if you don't like it, sooner or later it will get to you if you don't tell people because if they see no wrong in it, they'll keep doing it.

OH... A mysterious name, hmm... well, your name can't be too long considering it is pretty short scribble in length. So, I'm assuming your name is either somewhere between 3 to 5 letters. The dot has a lot of variables.

However, I am thinking that you overcompensated so that you could make your name look larger than actually, it is. So, I'm going to assume your name is 3 letters long. I guarantee without you telling me... I'll figure your name out in a couple of days without having to ask you... or without you having to say to me personally.

I'll keep it between us that you may have vouched your name earlier than expected. However, if I get your name wrong when I mention it, I'll give you something very crucial about me that might be able to pinpoint you to who I am.

Deal? Except, I am not giving... yet.

. . .

OH RIGHT, a thing that makes me angry. A buffering symbol that takes forever on a video... now that is enough to infuriate someone.

Q1. What is your favorite band or singer?

A1. I don't like pop music, either... I love experimental music, I suppose. I adore music that speaks a lot of volume without a lot of words if you get my drift. One of my current favorite artists is a guy called Olafur Arnalds, that guy is pretty talented. My favorite song from the guy right now is called 0952. You should check out the video if you like Classical, it has a beautiful meaning. How about you what is your favorite artist?

Q2. What is my favorite childhood memory?

A2. I really liked it when my father and I used to build large structures from Lego. We don't really do it anymore because you know I've gotten older, but I'd still like to do it sometimes. But of course, my dad is getting older, and preferences have changed so... that's that.

YOUR LETTER WASN'T corny at all... it went swimmingly. I guess you'll see this letter tomorrow... and I'll probably get mine the next because it'll probably take you a while to reply to me if you're going to the doctors to have your knee checked out, and I don't know what day that will be... so what day are you going to the doctors?

Until next time,
    Sherlock

ENTRY #17

To Sherlock,

PHEW... that's great to hear, I hate putting off your messages when I know I receive them. It makes me feel like I am letting you down even if I am super busy.

Yet, while I plan to get back to your letters, it appears to me every time I do, it is like half a century. Therefore, if I take longer to get a response from, don't sweat it, I just have a lot of my plate.

How DID the dentist get on? I avoid the dentist at all costs if I can help it. I loathe getting injuries in sports in case my teeth start bleeding or something. Except, I guess I can't complain if I have a nice set of teeth due to the visits.

Anytime I envision dentistry, I always picture an unhinged man pulling out my teeth with pliers and suturing them to another person's gum line with fish wire, and my pearly whites dangling down into a toothless mouth.

Yep... let's scratch such a thought that is the number one reason I avoid those clinics. Plus, to make matters worse, I can imagine a deranged woman is supporting his sickness lol. I think that is the reason I don't eat a lot of sweet stuff, and as to why I brush my teeth three or four times a day. I know it's probably weird, but I bring my toothbrush to school. I know... I need to stop lol.

NATHAN BRIAR PLAYS a safety defense in football. Typically, Nathan is extra cautious about his appearance and how his actions are perceived. I could not help but laugh out loud to his blunder. I don't talk all that much to the guy, just Nathan is cool enough to have a conversation with in the moment.

After the indecent, Nathan did not get all pissy and shit. The guy laughed it off. Somehow, his self-ridicule was extra amusing more so than the combustion happening in the lab.

Honestly, I have no clue what we were supposed to be doing, other than the point the teacher made after the big ordeal. Except, yes, I had a crazy, bizarre day. I surmise you're right, it's not cool watching people get hurt but then again, I guess I don't care as long as it doesn't come back to hurt me.

I'm not trying to be insensitive here, but I don't see why I should concern myself worrying about other people considering it's not going to get me anywhere in the long run. If they are my immediate family or friends then, of course, I will care, but if it directly confronts me in my everyday life then, of course, I'll have to deal with it.

I ASSUME you find the statement amusing, considering I

have no guts to stand up to my dad for bullying me or to the guys on the team. I reckon the word brave does not apply to me. I pretend to be somebody else when I am not feeling myself.

I can't explain it; except, it draws attention from people, and I think that is the answer to the question. I am trading the real me for recognition.

Yet, I have gotten used to being in the limelight, I can no longer understand why I continue to act. I think I have forgotten how to stop.

ODDLY ENOUGH, the caretaker and I had a run-in today, again. Except, it was not after hours. Around lunch, I bumped into the guy while on my way to the cafeteria.

The dude pulled me aside and asked to speak to me. Here I am thinking, what did I do now? Though, the man appeared to be overly friendly today.

ANYWAY, the caretaker directed me toward a wall in the corridor, so the two of us would not add to the congested traffic heading for the cafeteria. The man apologized to me about our run-in; he said he was very sorry for being crabby with me.

The other thing is the man appeared to be genuine. I did not know how to handle the odd encounter. So, I told him it wasn't a big deal. I legitimately shook hands with the caretaker and went on my way.

I have been pondering the moment most of the afternoon: trying to evaluate what it means. Only, anytime I try to arrive at a conclusion, the idea has already bounced ahead.

. . .

I currently have a free class, and I am writing a letter at the back of a free class since the teacher is in a meeting. Thank God for no substitutes... and always when there is no teacher to direct the class, nobody dares go to the office to report that a supervisor has not shown up.

I wonder if it is alright to take letters home for the weekend, and pen them there and return the messages on Monday. Almost every Friday I have trouble getting around to replying back to you; it's something I want to do, just I have other obligations of a Friday afternoon. I think I'm going to ask my teacher if I can take my Friday letters home with me so that I can still write to you. Not every day is going to be as handy as today is. Typically, when I sit down to compose another note... class is out, and the teachers want me to leave. I know it's a funny thought. Most people, when they reach the end of the week, all flow out the doors from school and work. However, I... I choose to stay on because you're like the only one I can be honest to... and I don't want to miss the opportunity to tell you about my day... or hear about yours.

I get headaches when I am under pressure, so maybe you are stressed. Possibly take some time off and recuperate. You can rest for both of us.

Indeed, living in your head is not good. At times I do feel like I'm the only one who understands all my problems, and I have never met anybody else who seems to have the same profound effect as you do. It's like so easy to talk about pretty much anything... I don't even know you. I mean, I know who you are as a person.

Well, I'm getting a real gist of the type of person you are. When you overthink, does your head feel like it's melting from the inside out? Yet, at the same time, there is like this peculiar pressure pressing down on the top of your head.

I get those too... my mom once said its tension, not sure what that means, but I haven't got a lot to be tense about.

Can you be tense without having anything to be anxious about? However, I've never had a headache that's been so bad that it hurts my eyes, maybe you should get checked by the nurse or go to a doctor. My cousin wears glasses... and sometimes when she doesn't put her glasses on while watching tv or reading, she gets terrible headaches. I'm presuming you don't wear glasses, maybe it could be to do it your eyesight. I'm no doctor, of course, I'm just offering another opinion.

I just remembered it considering you said you have headaches and, well my cousin gets headaches when she doesn't wear glasses.

FIXATION on a particular subject I can relate to. After all, my entire life revolves around sports and making my dad happy. Therefore, trying to make everyone happy is my fixation. I can't say I get headaches from being overly obsessed with a specific subject. I tend to feel very toxic. Sometimes when I am under pressure, I get very grumpy, and my chest feels tighter. It's almost as if somebody is winding a rope around my chest, and every time a revolution is complete, they pull it tighter to the point it feels like my insides are being squished together. I haven't told anybody about that particular sensation, but I have googled it a couple of times, and anytime I search about it in various forms, my diagnosis appears to be anxiety. It's not a pleasant feeling, I always feel stressed and undervalued, but still I carry on, not that I am sad or anything, but it would be nice to be able to wake up in the morning and not feel a pent-up awareness that I will have to face my father at the breakfast counter before school.

Is it possible to get trapped by something you inherently like? I have heard about people who get so caught up in what it is they are doing they forget about people who often matter the most. Is that how some people become workaholics and forget about family? Is it them just caught up in a responsibility that they are obligated to complete their tasks by home time, and family comes last.

OKAY, here's the condition, science is not my thing. I have never been good at it. I tend not to waste any time trying to better myself with that particular subject in school, I don't see the point. I have tried in the past, but it just doesn't seem to work, I can't wrap my head around certain things... Or most things.

Yeah, talking about water is the sub-par for a boring conversation if you ask me. Sorry, it's just that is what I'd expect a stereotypical geeky, nerdy guy from the 1980s to start talking about. Not that you are nerdy or geeky, but my suspicions are that you are, not that anything is wrong with it.

God, this sounds pathetic... don't it. I'm trying to make a statement while being pessimistic and both optimistic. I guess I am a go with the flow sort of guy. I don't believe patience has anything to do with getting ahead.

ON THE CONTRARY, I have to say that not having some

patience has always worked out in my books. People are still out saying things will come to those people who wait... the perception is wrong... Nothing will come to you if you abide with time. The past is there to haunt you... but waiting won't bring you anywhere. So, if you want something you have to go after it.

No offense, but who wants to talk about depressing stuff all day? It's a lot easier to ask about the weather than it is to debate why you think Donald Trump is in the White House. Topics like the weather, sports, and movies are always a lot easier to approach than serious problems. The world is littered with enough hard-core shit, that people just want to escape. No wonder books, movies, and video games are some of the best forms of escapism. They are simplistic since many can use it. Folks just like an uncomplicated escape; the pressures of reality do clog up from time to time. I understand what you mean by not wanting to chat about stuff that is not as engaging; though trust me on this.

If you're going to make some half-decent friends, you have to be willing to compromise and talk about other things that are not science. Whenever I'm with my friends; I speak about whatever it is they want to talk about, and on occasion, I inject some material I want them to hear.

TO BE honest with you I have never played Dungeons & Dragons, it's not my thing. Not that I would be unwilling to learn how to play, but have you ever thought that some people may not like board games.

Perhaps a person you want to get to know is an outdoorsy person. How would that make you feel if you're an outdoorsy person? Plus, I'll make sure to remember if I see a person mumbling to themselves along the corridors knowing that it is you.

I NEVER SAID you were terrible... not at all. I presume that you didn't go around trying to cause trouble, I was just kidding before. So, does that mean you're calling me mundane? Except, if you can make that explosive diarrhea work, then I want in. The only question is what teacher do we target?

When you said that you may be in trouble, I picture you hanging upside down in the Penguins lair in the bowels of Gotham city. No offense it gave me a chuckle, however where the thing gets weird is when I showed up in a Catwoman outfit to save you, we both got strung up. I have no idea why..., the scenario is pretty amusing if I must say so.

Is that how you describe yourself... Goody-goody shoes? I hold my hands up and say I'm not a problem child. I have had my fair share of detentions, and I have been written up for misconduct, some vandalism, and profanity. Oh, and truancy, well that's what the principal calls it. Why can't she just call it what everybody else calls it... It's ditching.

The way you mention your academic life always makes you sound like you are this unbelievable sensational person. I try to be everybody's friend in school, and I'm a lot noisier when I'm not at home. I think I suppress myself the moment I put the key in the front door of my house, knowing that dad might be around.

If you are using the carbon footprint statement as a way to describe your existence, then I assume I have a similar situation. Often I feel like my skin is scaffolding, and inside its hollow. The only time I act out is when I'm trying to impress people or get them to notice me. It's not every day I go out of my way to try and make people like me, but when I do, I end up going the extra mile. At certain points in my life, it has got me into trouble, I have a habit of not thinking before I do something.

FOR A MOMENT THERE, I was going to ask what your lab partners name was. Except, I remembered that we are not supposed to give our names even though I probably gave you my name by accident... I'm not sure.

Is it weird that for once that if I were to do science, I'd like to have you as my partner? I know I said before I'm not interested in it all that much; except, sometimes I just want to learn. I know it makes me sound stupid, though I feel dumb. So, I suppose the best way I can try to make up for that is to be willing to listen, to try and understand.

Only, when my best friend sits beside me for science, I can't concentrate. My friend is always talking, and half the time, I miss what the teachers are doing. If I had the chance to be your science partner, I say that would be pretty cool. You'd probably tell me to shut up if I start talking, and just to focus.

Whereas that would be a great thing, I think. At least in some way, I'd be trying to learn. It's funny how both of us have two completely different perspectives on the same situation. When you say that you wish something could change, I seem to want what you have. Also, when you declare that you want things to change, it seems to appear in my life.

Do you think it's fate that the two of us have been assigned to one another? Do you think it's a chance that I just pulled your number out of a container? Honestly, I think the both of us were paired up for a reason, it's comforting... you know. Maybe in the future, we can consider switching lives for the day.

Ms. Byrne is a nice teacher, though I don't think she has the finesse as you have stated... whatever that word means. Personally, I reckon I'd rather a teacher from our school to take the position, instead of a new arrival. You never know what an outside party might be like. They could be disastrous for our school, could even make life hell for everyone within the building. Well yeah, most teachers when they advance up the ladder, they are going to have to act more professional.

Though it's not just teachers, the more promotions you get theoretically it means you have to work more professional, rigid and un-fun. Perhaps it's a technique applied to be able to demand respect or attention from an entire faculty and a body of students. The stress I can believe would be crippling.

As a way to enforce some form of mutual respect, the principle must apply this airy demeanor so that people do not take advantage of their generosity while in a leading position. I've never thought about an achievement like this; I figure it is true, we rip out contents of value to believe we are better or cured.

If there is a vote for being the president or you know... the guy who runs everything for the club I vote you. I know you'd do an excellent job at it. Do you have anything specifically you want to do? There is no point in applying for or getting nominated if it is something you do not care about.

Maybe there will be a meeting where everyone will sit down and discuss what has to happen, but as you said early days... eh.

Is it your first time to work with people like this? I'm not sure if you sound happy or slightly terrified... perhaps a mix of both? Just maybe pooling your efforts with a team will be beneficial, it will take you outside the comfort zone you have built concrete prison walls around.

I know the characteristics, it is weird to be proud of getting a position, but you are undecided personally as to whether you want to keep the job or not. Straying away from what you are comfortable with is a sure way to note that you are growing up... at least that's what our health teacher says.

I DO KNOW what it feels like to sit in the reception area for hours. Worst of all is having to wait during lunch to see the vice principal when she is too busy snacking away on her meal. Since when does the world stop? It's ironic I am punished, and can't have my lunch, but she can have hers. I wouldn't say I'm a bad guy. Though, I do occasionally stir up some trouble. I guess that is a milestone for you to be able to tell you've met the vice principal for your behavior. The first time I saw the vice principal I was not rattling, I confess I was a little nervous... just a little... but that's between you and me okay.

I think I am a little sad now that you pointed it out more clearly. I don't like being mistreated, but evidently, it always appears to work out this way. And no, I don't tend to open up about my feelings much to anybody... On the contrary, you are one of the first people I've ever told. Actually, you are the only one. Thanks, man, it's good to know you have my back. Likewise, if you ever want to give the old shit a whirl to get it out of your system, I don't have a doctorate in psychology, but I'll listen.

MOM IS COOL AND ALL, after all, I love her, she's my mom. Except, as much as the woman goes out of her way to help me sometimes, it appears like our relationship lacks something. I don't know how to explain it; however, I don't know how I would be able to open up to my mother. I guess she is too preoccupied with other things for me to be able to sit down and cry figuratively. I'm not saying that she would turn me away, I believe she will listen, but again, I imagine it is something I'm not all that comfortable with.

I don't like causing problems for people. It is one reason why I don't go out of my way looking for help so that it doesn't wind up creating further difficulties for people. I reckon me talking about peer pressure with the team would go in one ear and out the other. Little pep talks don't matter when you're on the field, the only thing you want to do is win.

Nobody on the team will be willing to have a talk when you're running purely on adrenaline. I can even say that the coach would have a face on him if I mentioned that in the locker room. Boys are not supposed to have problems, that is why we are supposed to clear them up as quickly and as effectively as possible, and man up about it. Thanks, you're an awesome guy too.

IT'S okay you don't have to go out of your way to talk to counselors or whatever. I have a good feeling knowing that you're going to do it regardless of whether I ask you to or not. Therefore, fire away. I am beginning to value your advice, it's like you're a master at what to do next. How do I explain it? It's like you give me inspiration or motivation to create a new image of myself. Whenever you try to cheer me up you, you give me this warm feeling... I know... don't mention this to anybody else because it looks wrong when I write it. However, I've come to love talking to you. As I said you have my permission if you want to ask around on behalf of me but, yeah perhaps I should get into the habit of not sharing some sappy feelings with you. Only, I cannot help it, you are so easy to talk to.

Unfortunately for me, I seem to be in everybody's business. Perhaps I shouldn't have said that, but maybe that does go to show that I am in a position where people know me more often than not. On occasion, I feel flooded with the amount of attention I receive, and sometimes I forget there are people outside of all the adoration.

Meeting you has been awesome, I think for the fact that you are from a completely different background than I, has made it all worthwhile for the inconvenience. I'm not saying having to do this was an inconvenience, I'm just saying if it weren't for the hiccup at the beginning, then I would have never gotten the chance to become friends.

I think in the way of all the screw-ups I have made in the past, and all the things I failed to do, this is one thing I can say from the bottom of my heart I am proud I have done, even if at the start I wasn't all that proud, to begin with.

JUSTIN BLAKE IS A LIKABLE GUY; I doubt him being feminine would matter much. It's funny how you notice things when you take the time to observe them. That is if you are looking for what it is you are looking for. Many people will bypass ordinary things they see in a day without a second thought.

However, I noticed the little pieces, how his hands' gesture when he talks, how his eyelashes fluttered when he is nervous, how Justin scrunches up his face and crinkles his nose... everybody has a different coping mechanism. When you take the time to figure it out, you can talk to pretty much anyone when you solve it. It gives you another bargaining chip to have a conversation with. I think I've known Justin has been gay since the third or fourth-grade... I know that is a long time to be sure of his sexual preference, but when a kid goes around that flamboyant, I'm not exactly sure how you can miss it.

Plus, the kid talks about musicals all the time. Furthermore, it is plastered everywhere; on his social media platforms, school locker, his books. Everywhere. It's not hard to take a second guess at what it is he loves when he so freely places all of his interests in one basket. At first, I was nervous about approaching him to talk I mean, nobody in my position speaks about Glee or Broadway. Someone could get the wrong impression.

AFTER A WHILE, it will regularly wear you down. I can wake up every morning and play sports, but sometimes it just doesn't fulfil me. Every now and then you have to take a step back from what it is you like to evaluate where it is you want to go next with your hobby. When you spend too much time with your head up in the clouds. When it is time to descend, you are dazed and confused. All you have known while you're up there is the suffocating anxiety of wanting to come down. Seems like you have the right idea to step away occasionally. I have a hard time doing that. If I woke up in the morning and I did not have sports, I don't think I'd have anything to get out of bed for. I know that seems hard or maybe hash coming from me, whereas you would say I have everything I could possibly want, but sometimes I use sports as a distraction more than anything else.

You are right about rushing into choice after choice without pre-examining the judgment. I have plenty of uneducated decisions on my plate. Some I am proud of, and others I have just come to accept as if to say, 'oh well... it's not what I was looking for, but I'll settle for less.' One reason as to why people might not take the time to evaluate a decision is because the world is moving so fast. It's scary to slow down. Possibly people are afraid that if they stop in the ever-growing merry-go-round, they'll lose the pace and never be able to retain it.

I CAN'T SAY my introduction to Justin Blake wasn't one of my most valued achievements. Only, it worked, didn't it. I found an extended solution to an otherwise easy resolution when all along I could have just walked up to him and asked for the favor, but that's me I take the long route... scenic route. Glee is like your whole life is a musical, and if your life were a musical, it would be called Glee.

One reason I suppose I watched it was because it seemed so happy; I guess that's one thing about gay people... no matter the amount of crap that gets hurled at them, they pick themselves up: dust themselves off and keep on smiling, proud, determined that they have a place in this world. Me, however, I'm not so sure, I just never know how one can be that happy, yet be repressed. Maybe it's the hope... Yeah, hope.

I understand, no trouble. I know some people prefer to be on their own. I assume I'd go crazy if nobody talks to me tomorrow. It would be a weird dreamlike sequence where I'd wake up, and everybody is alienated toward me.

I assume I've gotten used to always having someone there, the attention, and if that were to disappear, I wouldn't even know where to start rebuilding. I have many companions in school; only I have two friends outside who I trust with anything. It may not be much more than what you possess, but one friend makes all the difference.

It's funny how I'm surrounded by hundreds of people daily. Yet when it comes down to the crunch, I only trust two. Therefore, having one friend is better than having no friend. Right friend?

I know it's going to be crazy for you when you start doing what it is you're doing, and I hope you don't forget about me in the process. I pray you don't get too busy that you won't find the time to talk to me. I'm glad I have been able to give you some confidence. I suppose, and in a weird way, you've made me feel better about myself. Do meet all the people you can... Life is for reaching out to as many people as you can and experience the wicked wild journey. Now I sound like some modern Indie who has yokel tendencies from Alabama. Plus, a side note I crawl out of bed every morning too... school is meh.

YES, okay dude we are past it. Honestly, sure. I am disappointed when he doesn't turn up. If he did, I don't know what I'd do. In a way, I guess it would be oddly satisfying. Knowing that my dad would be in the stands, of course, I'd play harder. I'll give it my all, and somewhere down deep inside of me, I will know that it will not be enough for my father. My dad is one of those guys, yet, I can't help but not try to be something in his eyes. I know it's foolish, I know I can't be helped or stopped. It's the only thing I know how to do, so I have to keep trying. As long as it takes... Right?

When I started lacrosse and basketball, there was nothing else in the world that could amount to the joy I felt and the escape of getting away from my everyday mundane life. It fixed me for a little while. I enjoyed doing sports every Tuesday and Thursday. I'd even go as far as to say, I was glad I was picked for the matches on the weekends. When I won them, I haven't got the words to explain how pleased I was.

Except, after a while, the novelty wore off. I wasn't getting the attention of the one person who mattered most to me. Soon sports became just an escape, but not so much an exciting adventure anymore. I just do it now so I can get out of the house, and sometimes I return feeling like my head has been cleared or weight has been lifted off my shoulders.

A game on the field gave me clarity, I didn't know I could possess. After a while, it faded out, and the lack of emotion I was experiencing turned to an anxious rage. I became a horrible person that nobody really liked on the field. Certified, I was a lot cockier and obnoxious, so much so other teams hated facing me. It got to the point my own team began to resent having me.

After a while I stopped being angry, people started to like me again, but I felt like something was missing. I still feel like something is absent. I did everything I possibly could just to make my dad see me, yet he never does. Dad always sees Jordan, and for a while, I hated my brother. I hated him, my own brother.

That was until I met you, and things started to get a little better. It's like you flicked a switch inside my head, and I chose not to want to hate Jordan anymore.

I'M TRYING to fix all the mistakes that I've done in the past, and it's hard, you know. Going to the top is what everybody wants to do, but you should try it just so you know how it feels. Before I started out with anything, I'd give just to be able to walk down the street or the corridors in school when nobody knew me. Being popular is not worth all the hysteria and aggravation. I feel trapped like I am molded into a specific image for people, and when I try to change people don't like it. All they see is this talented guy who has a lot going for him when all I crave to be is the friendly guy in the corner who doesn't hate his little brother.

I've been a real shitbag to some people who have been there for me, and all I have done for them is walk all over their generosity. I guess, when I woke up from my impermeable slumber, I realized I am not a nice person anymore. You know I don't want to be that person anymore. I just want to be... like you.

Man... you have got me on the verge of crying here but don't you ever tell anybody this; could ruin my rep. Though when we finish up with this assignment... please meet me... you know so I can thank you. I'll buy you a Coca-Cola or milkshake or hell a science beaker if that's what you so desperately want. I reckon I have lost what matters to me just because someone else is putting a damper on my dream. I shouldn't let their cloud put out the fire. I want to be able to wake up in the morning, and say I'm happy to be here... I don't have pockets of happiness like you described it when waking up happy; to love and feel loved. Though if an inkling of it were there, it ought to be enough.

. . .

I GUESS if you find my family fun, and I find your family captivating then I think we are both polar opposites. We do get on well, though. It goes to show that you don't have to have a lot in common to become friends with someone. If anything, maybe it's more of a benefit. With the two of us not knowing anything about each other or the past times we keep, it is all that more intriguing to learn something different.

Your mom sounds like the kind of woman I'd like to meet. She seems funny, and if it's any correlation, maybe she is a lot like you. If your mom is somewhat like you, then I guarantee I'd like her, just like how I've come to like you. At least your mom and dad see you; my mom is too busy with her magazines, and my dad... well, you know the drill.

I'VE HEARD THAT BEFORE; television rotting kids brains like termites. I don't think it is just that either. Your statement has some reasoning behind it. It seems that the medium is distracting, and I suppose that is the only reason why people use that metaphor. Why else would you want to do anything else if you're distracted by television... because it's easy?

The reason it is an easy distraction is that whatever you see on tv is simplified... whereas in a book or a puzzle... it's not as simple. There is a whole turn of events that you need to wrap your head around. Not that I read many books, but sometimes if I do try, I always find it weird when the author of the book is trying to talk to me as if they know me. I guess that's just style though. Screw tv and books... actually, Spotify is life.

. . .

THE THING IS I do view Jordan negatively when it comes to favoritism. As I said, I'm trying to be a better person. So, I have been gradually trying to make it up to my little brother. I know nothing will come of it... being nasty, but it's not like I have been ill-treating him. I've always approached Jordan reasonably.

It's just sometimes it's hard to do that when you have this little voice in the back of your head saying he's the favorite one. It's tough to ignore the sound and carry on as if nothing's the matter.

I don't think Jordan understands what dad and I are going through. In a sense, I feel sorry for Jordan, he is the odd man out. My little bro is in the middle of the crossfire, and Jordan can't help it. I guess your statement about being the chosen one is in its way a hard position to be in.

AT THE SAME TIME, I consider my situation is just as tricky if you're one of the most liked kids in town, and the relationship with your parent and sibling is affected. My family is all I have, and I feel guilty for having the thoughts I sometimes have. When I was younger, there were times when I wished they weren't my family. In the past, I wanted to be taken in by a new collection of people, just to be treated fairly or loved. Is that a crime?

I PRESUME my case doesn't just sit with my family. I assume many others experience the same problem. In a way, it is comforting to know I'm not alone. Unfortunately, what makes it even harder is the point in which Jordan tries extraordinarily hard to look up to me. It seems Jordan is asking for validation, and I guess I have never given him much. Perhaps I should learn to do it to make him happy for once.

Cool, that sounds pretty awesome. Does that mean your dad plays video games with you? If your old man has knowledge of how to fix a computer, surely, he can handle a console? At first, I didn't notice your statement about my dad. It stung a little, but hell... I'm used to it.

I know right it's scandalous, cheesecake and vanilla Oreo are yuck. However, I think I'm coming around to your way of thinking with the Hershey's chocolate, it's the best thing I've ever tasted. I got you there... You probably thought I was going to agree with you, but Hershey's chocolate is the worst thing ever.

Not to mention you do sound like you are the type to want exceptional quality goods. And no, I'm not saying Johnny Rockets is better than my mother's cooking. Everybody knows mom's food is the best. I don't know why I haven't thought of that, thanks for putting the idea in my head, I'll get a blender so I can make ice cream. If we ever meet one day, we so got to do this. Netflix, ice cream, and a comforter.

Who said I'm a natural pioneer, I'm terrible at directions. Leave me in charge of navigating in a car, and we'd end up in Los Angeles instead of New York. The good thing is though since the building is historical, it has to be on the web.

You can give me the coordinates, but I'm already going to say I found it. Possibly it's the same place, perhaps not let's see if I'm right... anyway, I hope I am correct, I'll be going there tomorrow.

I GUESS in a way I'm extending an invitation if you want to come along... I know we're not supposed to meet before the project is finished. Except they didn't precisely specify where you could and could not attend.

If you want to meet tomorrow, I can join you outside the front entrance to the building if it is inherently right. That would be so awkward if I got the thing wrong and you just stood outside waiting for me. I can imagine it would be a funny prospect... You'd be standing at one building, and me waiting at another. Remember, I am not forcing you to meet me, but it would be nice to figure out who I'm chatting with.

OUR LETTERS CONTINUE to grow lengthy. I am half figuring whether I should cut this letter into two portions, but then I'd have to wait to tell you the rest, so I just keep going.

SUPERHERO MOVIES HAVE ALWAYS BEEN full of innuendos. Except, now it is more universal. It is amusing to see a guy in tight yoga pants prancing across the screen, getting the shit knocked out of him. Deadpool is pretty good... I guess that fits the bill.

Naturally, Ryan Reynolds is funny, so I don't see why not... milk it for all it's worth. I don't think it's just Netflix, however, pumping out in 80s vibe. I think people are just getting a little vintage. The other day I saw a girl wearing this old faded looking retro Adidas jacket. The thing looked older than my mom... but the weird thing about it was it seemed pretty good if I must say so.

CURIOSITY I THINK IS what starts most adventures. It's like a ping going off in your brain when you find out you can be profitable from an idea you'll enjoy that's when things start to become business.

NOBODY WANTS to wait in line, so naturally, everybody wants to cut in front. All money begins with a proposition, that's when the real human element of monopoly comes into play.

I think I know the voice you are describing. The "*what if*" sound always seems to want me to explore an idea or examine another part of me that I never knew was there, but yet at the same time, I'm afraid of taking that step.

I RECKON many people are like "*what if...*"

WHAT IF I possessed this life or their life? Or if I did this instead of that. It is sad a lot of people don't see through this element. So many settle for less, and we try to comfort ourselves with another alternative means for the more significant measures we wish we could've had.

From now on, I think I'm going to follow the "*what if* voice...*" since I have met you, I have been only supporting it, and I feel a lot better. I am even happier and more together. I guarantee if I told my friends, they'd probably say, "what the hell are you smoking."

. . .

EXCEPT, if I ever have kids one day I'll try to teach them to follow the voice so many do not listen to. Many people I think are given the motivation, but they don't act on it straight away. Folks let it brew and fester. You'll never reach your potential if you never try or follow the encouraging voice in your head. It's nice to know that I'm not the only one who has it, the only question I have is what does everyone's voice sound like. To me, my voice whispers like a man in his mid-thirties. At the heart of it, the guy craves understanding, and perhaps the person is a little naïve.

WHAT DOES your voice appear like... not your actual voice, but you know... the sound everybody subconsciously hears inside their head? I guess the noise can be anybody or anything you want it to be... So who is yours?

I THINK we need above all is to reestablish some form of originality to bring back the novelty value. We have forgotten what is meaningful and honest, and in a way, we have marginalized ourselves for the sake of comfort. Except, the word comfort I'm assuming will mean something different to everybody. The example is which is the right comfort, and what is wrong.

OF COURSE, I heard you cuss, you can't wiggle out of this situation so easily... I'm joking. I presume I am turning into a mini-you. Don't get your hopes up just yet. You might set yourself up for disappointment, but if you stick with me, I'll get you to the path of treachery lol. I guess I'm having a bad influence on you then if you are using profanity. And there it goes, why would I ever use the word profanity... Shit, I just said it again didn't I? Is this how it might work by the end of our letters? Me becoming you; and you- me?

ALASKA... *check, check, check, check*... I'm building my log cabin there or perhaps somewhere far from civilization in Canada. I'm sure you will get the chance to travel after you leave school. Neither have I been to Alaska so, you can count me in, I'm there. Just let me know so I can start saving. I reckon it will be disastrously expensive. Traveling in pairs is always a richer experience than doing it solo. Just had a weird reminder when Yolo was a thing... sorry I couldn't help it.

Yeah, Barren... I guess your words are rubbing off on me. Let's get one thing clear. I don't have everything figured out, but I do have ideas of where I wish to go.

For one, I don't want a scholarship to do with sports. I want to study music... that is a lot harder and weirder to say than I care to admit. Legitimately, my heart is feeling all weird and crazy in my chest right now.

YEAH, dad and I were close when I was younger, we both know how the relationship turned out. I have heard when a new baby is brought into the house, parents' attention is typically turned to the youngest child. I don't or never expected any more or less. Only, Jordan is old enough now so it would be nice if my folks separated that love and attention.

You know what? It's handy having you around. I never

thought of asking my dad to watch westerns with me, perhaps I'll work up to it, so thanks.

INSTEAD OF SITTING HERE day after day regurgitating crap that we'll never use, why don't we try and fight for change. You know like to ask for more freedom within the school structure... like we can still have basics like learning how to read and write, not forgetting math.

However, wouldn't it be nice to be able to grow and develop skills we are naturally attuned to, rather than trying to improve skills we'll never be good at? That's like telling a person who is good at carpentry to design project runway apparel... or even making a video game from scratch.

THE WORLD IS OVERPOPULATED, there is no room for individuality anymore every position has been filled, every idea thought, practically everything built.

I'm scared of the way the world is heading. I mean it looks pretty awesome in video games and movies, you know the futuristic prospect, where cars are flying or not. You get the drill, how everything is nearly animatronic, though people will have no jobs.

Everything is done by machine. We have reached the point where we have created something far more fundamentally superior than us. Perhaps we've gotten too intelligent, people would probably say there's no such thing as being too clever, but when you have many minds working to this dream, things are going to start changing pretty fast, and not all for the better.

. . .

I RECKON what you say is true, we teach humans how to behave. It's ironic how our own system is also the same system that corrupts everything. This is probably going to sound poetic as well but is man supposed to be confined or are we supposed to be able to roam free. I guess if our population were much smaller, we wouldn't have to resort to such a system. However, we have been brainwashed to a certain degree without even realizing it. What you say is true when you really think about it. Many people will put it down to beliefs or self-interests.

Except, many people don't seem to understand that they are a cog in a machine, and that's a scary thought. I am a cog in the engine, and so are you, the teachers, my dad, everybody. Do you think the men and woman who are unintentionally brainwashing would change their ways if they knew what it is they are doing? Somehow, I think we have evolved so much that if we tried to switch direction, it would mean the end for us. I presume it's one of those things that you have to wait until the collapse is upon us finally to find out how much we screw things up.

FOR AS LONG AS I can remember, every history book claims the same thing; they always want the best for the people, when the people are the problem.

Nobody goes out of their way to cause trouble for a particular reason, not even for the sake of war. They want what's best for the people, and ordinary folks don't matter much when you can have the best of the people.

I never gave much thought into what it is I want to be when I grow up, I mean I've thought a little about doing architecture. Though that was before I sure... you know Pre-K crap. Music is my dream now, I know I'd be safer doing architecture. Only the world needs more farmers... Not musicians... though I can be both.

If you focus on the unnecessary, that is what makes the average person. What defines great men and women, is they didn't pursue the useless. Those folks never even flinch thinking about working a dead-end job; they took the plunge and went for the kill. The people worked hard and tirelessly on what it is they wanted, and even if it's not the most direct route for most, it pays off after a while, even if it takes years.

A dead-end job has no place for people with a plan, I don't think you can put experience on paper, but in the modern world, it seems to be the case that you can put expertise down on paper. I surmise there is an irrationality to this concept, as we can learn anything we put our mind to, given a chance to learn something anybody can do it. I never knew you needed a degree in brewing coffee to just become a barista. And yes, that was a joke *hardy-har-har*.

My knee is still a bit banged up but, I'll get over it now I think. I don't exactly want to know what's inside my leg, I am already squeamish when it comes to horror movies. Though I have heard about kneecap disintegration with athletes. I hope that's not the case with me, I'd like to be able to play for a lot longer. I am getting my leg checked out, so I'll get back to you on that when it is done. The good news is; however, I didn't have to wear a strap today, so I guess things are looking up for me.

People who lose the power of their legs are brave, I don't

know how I will be able to manage if that happened to me. There are still so many places I'd like to see and explore. To actually be able to climb the side of the hill I'm traveling, there are just no words for that feeling. There is a sentiment that comes along with it announcing that you have done it, and I think those words have never been created yet.

PLAYING lacrosse with a strap is not too bad, I've gotten used to it, so it's no sweat. I'm hoping that the swelling goes down before another game night. However, I have the unsavory luck of being able to heal just in the nick of time before I actually have to play. When all along, I am worrying about whether or not I will be able to play the day before. Yet, when I get the all-clear, I can't sum up the sensations my body feels when I hear those words, "*You Can Play*."

SO, you have a low chill type of voice, I've gone through the full voice breaking procedure then. I know people get it at certain times; my cousin had a squeaky voice for almost a year and ½, I always find it funny because he sounded quite mature, but had a squeaky voice of a 12-year-old. The worst part was he was nearly 16.

I presume I am a master at burning people now... okay, that came off sounding a lot more sinister than I initially intended.

What I mean is, I'm good at coming up with quick one-liners that are sarcastically pleasing. And ain't that the truth, a dollar for every time our grandparents tried to tell us that we are an ungrateful or a degenerate generation, I'd be able to fill an empty swimming pool.

Legitimately when we meet someday, you have to show

me this pocketbook with all these quotes. Perhaps, I'll be able to steal a few if that's not too cheeky to ask. I reckon both of us are similar to each other in more ways than one. I have to say I do learn some insults from the web too, so, that in the hopes someone will piss me off, I will be able to repeat what I learned. Now that is a good use of study time.

No, I don't believe I'd take the limelight away from my little brother, that's a horrible and selfish thing to do. I can't say I'd leave my little brother exposed out in the open like a lamb to a slaughter. If Jordan did something wrong. Even though I'm having mixed feelings about Jordan, I'd still be there for him if he wanted me to be there that is.

I wouldn't say Jordan has been given a silver spoon, but he does have things slightly more comfortable than I. I don't believe he has to try as hard to please people because he doesn't have anything to hold or maintain.

Jordan is just a kid who plays sports on the weekdays and hangs out with his friends on the weekends. For me, most of the time, I'm practicing to try and get better. Jordan doesn't have to worry, I do. Sometimes all I wish I could do is walk away and go on vacation. Except, there's the word all the adult love to use... responsibility.

I couldn't imagine doing 50 years, and not liking what it is I do. I want to be able to enjoy every moment of my time on this planet. So, even if it is the wrong move financially, I want to be able to do something that makes me happy even if I have to sacrifice other alternatives.

Though you're right, money should not be the only reason why you choose to do something. Many people do that, they presume cash is a valuable asset when it's not, it's the passion.

The thing is I'm afraid to make the jump of being the talented kid on the team, to being a lonely boy playing on a stage in front of an entire school with only a piano as my friend. Sometimes when I play, I often feel naked... not in an actual sense, but I feel exposed, vulnerable, and warm at the same time. It's like I float, as you mentioned earlier. If you do decide to meet me at the weekend, please don't let my real image put you off. I know I'm the last person on earth ever to look like I enjoy classical music. Only, the medium frees my mind, and I can't say no to the bittersweet melodies of classical.

HALLOWEEN USED to be a fun time for me, I don't do it anymore. I used to go trick-or-treating with Jordan when he was little. I felt proud of leading Jordan house to house to get his candy. It was something I was good at or at least I knew I could do. For a moment, I always meant something to him. Even if the experience was immaterial to him, and the only thing on his mind was to gain candy, Jordan's company is what I appreciated.

It's like you're reliving my childhood when the family sat down and did something like a family ought to do. The only time we are all sitting in the same room as one another now is Thanksgiving... We've gotten so caught up in our own lives. We forget to share a little more of ourselves around to the ones who matter.

ACQUAINTANCES WILL WALK in and out of your life, but the person sitting across from you at the table on Thanksgiving is not always going to be there. I remember a while back grandma used to come to our house for dinner.

Except, her chair is filled now with my uncle. In my mind, the chair my uncle sits in will always be my grandmother's. We take so little care of the ones who matter anymore for the ones who are only a blip on our compass. I should really take my little brother out on an adventure this weekend to apologize for all the years I've been shitty to him.

Even though I probably haven't been shitty. Is that weird, apologizing for something you might not have done, but have felt... like my life is one never-ending apology, and at this rate, I don't know what it is I am apologizing for.

I THINK I BETTER GO, I'm getting a little soft talking about my feelings, and I don't want to show my true colors. I don't like them, so why would anybody else. Plus, you can't say I didn't give you a fair hint with who I am. My real name is Max... feels weird being exposed. I am unsure if this is a good idea, although at least you know my name.

I NEED to go so I can feel good again.

LATER,
 Watson

ENTRY #18

To Watson,

It's okay I don't expect an immediate reply, people get busy, things happen, therefore, no hard feelings. Plus, I am assuming your life is more complicated than mine. You have so many more people to spread yourself around to, and I know I'm only one person in your pond or sea... perhaps the ocean. I have no idea how large your body of water is.

The dentist was okay, everything's good. I don't have any new surprise cavities that need filling. I got my mom to make me an appointment so that I can be confident that my teeth were fine. The other night one of my incisors was a little painful.

Consequently, I wanted to check. I've never been a fan of dentistry's either. I don't mind having to sit in the waiting room, or having them stick a tiny mirror or a sickle probe into my mouth. I've always been relaxed when reclining in one of the chairs. The only thing I still find weird is having to look up the nose of the person, or when they look down at me directly in the eye.

Is it weird for Nathan Briar not to get all pissy and shit? Just asking, I don't associate myself with him, so I'm curious. Only, I reckon the sight to see was hilarious when it happened, too bad it didn't happen in one of my science classes.

It's never nice to see people get hurt. However, when watching YouTube videos, I'll make an exception. It's hilarious to watch some crazy lady or guy go off on a tangent when they don't get their own way.

They brought it on themselves. Once I saw this crazy lady who stole a kid's bike, it was comical. I wish I could remember the name of the video, except, the knowledge escapes me.

Maybe paying attention from now on in class before you do a demonstration will be useful. I wouldn't want to hear about a student inadvertently blowing himself up; only to find out it was you who wasn't paying attention to what you are mixing in the science beaker. We all should feel concern and worry for other people, we have lost an appeal to that emotion or connection.

Some people will take advantage of that commodity more than I'd like to admit. I have been a victim of their unfortunate act, and it has left me feeling a little worthless. I surmise there are worse things to fear than being helpful to someone rather than not being nice. The moment you start to stand up for other people, then you'll stand up for yourself.

I have found in the past by making the hard choices other people do not wish to take, I learned to grow and adapt myself and, in a way, it has helped me to take the leap for some choices I wouldn't have chosen otherwise. The first step in solving any problem is admitting that there is one. Brave can come in so many flavors that when you agree to make a change that's the real act of bravery.

The real you is far more exciting and entertaining then who I suspect you are. That's right, Max... I read all your letter first. However, I surmised who you were before you even told me. You left very little to the imagination, and I have been able to make a pretty educated guess on your identity. Even without your name being added to the document I sort of knew who you were talking about.

Plus, I know what you look like, and you are the last person I'd expect to like classical music. It's true, but that doesn't matter you're an awesome person on the inside and that's all that should matter. I can see why sometimes you feel crowded with all the attention. Now don't take this the wrong way, but you're a pretty good-looking guy, girls are going to be all over you... not metaphorically speaking.

You know what I mean. Except, I do pity you in a sense considering that's only one aspect of your life entirely. You are a jock, you're going to have a large gathering of girl supporters, fans, and sponsors at your back for most of your high school career.

They'll want you to go on to university, but I recall seeing you at the school talent show last year playing the piano accompanying some girl who I can't remember what her name was, but you still go a mile because your popular.

. . .

Perhaps sports is not what it is you are supposed to be doing; music is what you ought to be producing. When you start believing what you are lying about, that is when you begin trading a special part of you.

Nobody else can make up your mind, that is all you. No one in the world gets to decide whether you should be traded for another person unless you choose to let yourself fall helplessly into this trap.

Choosing to stop is hard, the act of stopping is not. It's just whether you want what it is you desperately need to be able to want to stop. I only have one question for you. What are you so afraid of? You have everything at your feet, and I don't believe your father is a source of fear for you when you want to make up your mind.

It makes you seem like the type of person who is a go-getter when you put your mind to it. It almost feels weird calling you Max after I've been calling you Watson for so long, but why are you so afraid to show the soft side of you to anybody else like you've done here with me. In a way, your words have been warm and homely to me. I'm not sure if that's much coming from a lonely nobody who roams the halls as if he doesn't exist, just eventually, there will come a time that you wished you had stopped trading yourself for a false person and it will be too late.

I have never pretended to be anything less than I am, I guess I'm just ashamed of my particular problem. Only, I have never hidden it in plain sight for everybody to see, I think even you have seen me. I'm that one kid that's everywhere but is never seen. So, do yourself a favor, stop pretending... don't settle for the role of something you have no passion for, aim higher.

You see, I told you the caretaker wasn't all that bad; his bark is much worse than his bite. Sometimes we make the wrong assumptions of people when they're having a bad day. I'm not condoning actions from certain individuals when they're having a defective day that it is good or acceptable to be able to berate someone. Sometimes people are so overworked and have very little respect that; all it could be is just a bad day. Perhaps the caretaker has no double meaning to his apology, maybe he just meant sorry, and that's all there was to it.

Lucky you, I don't ever get any free classes. Our teachers are punctual and have a groundbreaking level of attendance. Hell, I don't believe I've had a substitute teacher since third grade, now that's a long time. I can't remember what it is like to have a class that is not supervised, but it sounds cool and mystic as if I'd enjoy it if I got to experience it. If I do have a free moment I'm usually in the library, that's where I spend most my time anyway. I've been wondering the same thing whether I can take your letters home and return them on Monday.

I don't see why we'd have to ask for permission? I highly doubt having to ask, although, I guess there could be worse things than taking home our classwork to actually do it. Except, the assignment has gotten way out of proportion, and I no longer care about the grade I'm getting any more. I remember you asked me if I could help you with your grade and we've never implemented that into our letters. We became friends instead, and that's better than any category I can ever achieve.

I DON'T DO TOO WELL with having breaks. Anytime I take time off to recuperate, I find myself overthinking. Nothing would please me more than to have a vacation in the middle of school for both of us, but the sad reality is if I did, I'd feel more inclined to ponder choices I wish I could be doing or could have done or a tidbit of both.

Perhaps next week I'll take your letter home so that I don't have the stress of having to reply to your note before the school closes for the evening on a Friday. I've been getting headaches a lot lately, and I think it's down to stress.

Reasonably, I don't give my brain a minute to relax when most people don't use their head as much as I do. Sometimes when all you do is think, it gets very noisy inside your head. I used to have mind splitting migraines when I was about 10. I'm so thankful that I don't get them sort of headaches anymore. After a while, my mom took me to the hospital to have an MRI, yet everything seemed okay upstairs.

IT'S RATHER peculiar considering after the little scare, I picked up a book and studied the brain. It's hard not to want to know what is wrong with you, and the ironic part is I contributed to more headaches by stuffing piles of information into my head. I suppose I feel at home in my own world, and even I forget to tell myself to take a break.

You have no idea how good it feels to be able to walk out into the street and pass under a tree. The experience is weirdly cratonic and profound in a way I'd never envisioned a tree. Just thinking about the wind lazily flooding through the thick branches and brush makes me think of a warm sunny day, and somehow that eases my mind.

Yes, my head feels like it's melting from the inside out when I have too much on my plate. The odd thing is I never see the warning signs, I'll keep pushing until it's too late and I start to feel a tingling sensation at the top of my head. The sentiment you are feeling is tension, I don't know how to describe it clearer than that. I've had that feeling a lot, and I think it's better than having a migraine even though it's uncomfortable. Perhaps we should learn to take it easy every once in a while... although for me, I know it is going to be extremely hard considering when I know there is a problem I research the issue.

I believe you can be tense without having anything to be anxious about. Sometimes you can have an overwhelming sense of drowning I guess I ought to say. You might feel like everything is closing in on you, and you have much to do, but you're not making any leeway. It could be possible that you have anxiety attacks. Mind you; my headaches don't hurt my eyes all the time, it's only sometimes. And no... I don't wear glasses before you ask, nor do I look like Harry Potter, Velma Dinkley or Milhouse from The Simpsons.

FROM THE SOUNDS OF IT, you do have anxiety attacks or anxiety in general. The way you describe the winding rope around your chest and shortness of breath. I don't know any other symptoms that give it away as quickly and sufficiently as shortness of breath, and to the point, you feel like you're panicking. My family knows about nearly every medical condition I've had.

My parents know about my headaches, and I get

checked up regularly to make sure it's nothing like a tumor or crap. However, I suppose it's comforting knowing that everything is okay. People don't seem to mind it; it's a normal thing, you know. My brain overcooking is probably the equivalent to your knee giving out. You shouldn't feel embarrassed if you feel like you're under pressure.

You'd be surprised how willing people will be to help you out if you admit that you need help. I know this is not an AA meeting, I'm just saying when you say they need help with things someone will always be there. Yes, I think it is very plausible to get trapped by something you like. I don't know how to show the evidence that is right in front of us, but we are living proof that our condition exists.

Perhaps that's what it is we need to escape from our everyday lives like science and sports. Therefore, I have a new idea to break the ice. I'll just throw in a couple of things that could be of use for us to get to know each other.

The other day I was looking at my bucket list, and I concluded why not ask you what is on yours. What is it you would like to do in your lifetime. Think of 10 different things you would love to do and let me know. Mine are as follows,

1. Skydiving.
2. Invent the time machine to go back and meet Stephen Hawking.
3. Dogsled.
4. Visit Alaska.
5. I'd like to make a new best friend. My last BFF was an emo girl, but you know the two of us are far from each other now, so we drifted apart.
6. Learn to drive.
7. Again, my independence from my parents.

8. Star in a commercial.
9. Go to a paint party.
10. Last but not least, to bath in a hot spring in Iceland.

We all have our strengths and weaknesses; the main thing is if we decide to try it or not. Many people will give up because it's too difficult for them. I'd assume my reaction to restoring a car would be like you giving up science.

None taken, I presume if I were the stereotypical 1980s geeky guy, I'd be filthy rich by now. Except, most things have been figured, and now I have no idea why I have been placed on this planet. I firmly believe it all depends on what it is you are looking for. Some things require attention and patience, not everything can be rushed.

I'd love to be able to go with the flow, but I only can do that when I come from swimming and stop off at McDonald's on the way home to plug the gap in my stomach. If I were to rush into an equation in chemistry, there could be a lot of things that could go wrong or a simple error in the calculation could mean hours, weeks even loss of work. Knowing where it is you stand, and where you intend to go, bides your time. It helps you appreciate the time spent getting there.

I reckon what you have said holds a lot of truth, people find it easier to talk about the mundane stuff than complicated material. Being able to talk about pressing matters, I assume makes it viable to weed out the people who have no place to be able to discuss difficult issues. When most people are confronted with a hard choice, they conform or either get angry. Many people can try to radically look at the extremes on both sides of the fence. We need more people who can see on either side of the divide. Except, we have conditioned ourselves to separate that also. Either you are on one party or the other, or you're not on either side it at all.

Plus, if you try to point out something that the other side has correct and the other wrong, you are labeled a traitor. The world is a hard and scary place. Folks need to get used to this that things are not as how it seems in the movies. When you look at it, life is very dull and drab... the only thing we know how to do is violence because we respond to that so alarmingly brilliant that we crave to see more of this type of behavior. People will nod and say it's a terrible thing when an unspeakable act happens. Only people are also intrigued by the prospect that such a thing could happen. So, does that make us martyrs of our own free will? I assume it is one of the reasons why people vandalize.

HUMANS KNOW nothing else other than violence. So when you talk about it, it becomes an interest. The only reason our mediums of storytelling have disassociated from the harsh reality is that they are a distraction. When you think of it, every form of fairytale has some grisly back story or meaning to it.

Sleeping beauty is about rape. Little red riding hood, it's about a pedophile, Hansel, and Gretel, a cannibal.

The list goes on, humans like violent things and they would say they don't, but there are reminders of it everywhere no matter how far or distant you try and put yourself from it, the horrible intrigues us.

. . .

I PRESUME whenever you talk about movies or games, it's just another watered-down version of an old tale, that was shockingly horrific. People do bad things, stories give us the harsh truth, but in a diluted manner.

Do you think in the Roman age, seeing a head being chopped off would have been censored...? I don't think so. We hear of such stories in today's world, except not in exquisite detail. Yet, the condition of the head being chopped off still baffles us if we read it, witness it in a movie or hear about it.

NOT AT ALL, you are the last thing from mundane. I'll start concocting the plans right away, and explosive diarrhea will be made. Now, my kind sir, your question is admirable... who do we target? I'm kidding, of course... or am I? Muaha-hahahaha

HOW IS it I sound to you? Is it the pre-conceived disposition that I will not be able to take care of myself and that I'm some gimmicky sidekick, that the real badass has to come in and rescue me while I'm dangling 1 foot from the ground in the bowels of Gotham city.

Now I am intrigued... a Catwoman outfit seems fitting for your character. No wonder I turned up in a morph suit lol.

YES, I am Goody-goody shoes. Though, to state the obvious, you just contradicted yourself there. You said you're not a problem child, but you have been written up for misconduct, vandalism and what you have it. There's a word for that... an oxymoron... so now.

Yeah, I got a little antsy. I'm just trying to flaunt my intelligence, please ignore me. As a personal question, but what do you do when you skip school?

What could be so fun that you disappear for hours? Is it the thrill of knowing that you should be somewhere else and you are not, or is it just you feel like you have an understanding somewhere else?

ANOTHER QUESTION... what do you do when you ditch class?

Do you honestly think I'd make a good president of the student body? I find it difficult to find what pair of socks I'm going to wear every morning... and they're all white tube socks... I'm so bad at it; not that I don't care about it, just nervous. I'll get into it when I feel more comfortable around people. It does take me a while to warm up to folks I don't know.

I imagine it takes you next to nothing to know people considering you're so easy to talk to. I have never been in a group for pooling my efforts. It will be odd knowing I don't have to do everything myself. Plus, hello! Have you met me? Not officially, but I'm just saying here... I'm not the captain of a lacrosse team who has the most power of influence on the team.

How am I supposed to know what it's like to be in a specific position in such circumstances and understand what it feels like? I can only appreciate my accomplishments, not yours. But I'm not repeating this... well, I am... choose music.

. . .

SORRY, you feel like it is a one-sided relationship. Remember my emo friend I told you about earlier? Our friendship disintegrated to that sort of level that I no longer felt like I knew who she was anymore. I don't want to name names, I'm not that sort of person, but it was horrible not being able to trust someone I thought I could.

The bond I believe you are referring to is affection. Your mother could be less affectionate toward you. Perhaps she concludes you don't need to be babied or chaperoned because, in her mind, you have already reached a state of independence.

Some people are not the type to be able to sit down and cry with. I feel sorry for you, it seems you have nobody in your family you can talk to. Except, don't forget your little brother, you'd be surprised what stuff those guys come up with.

OFTEN AT TIMES we only have so many responsibilities to manage, sometimes folks are blindsided by what is essential. It could just look from the outside that your mother is too busy to talk to you. Only, I guarantee if you take the chance to speak to her, she will listen, mothers do.

Looking for help is not a crime, you know... you can ask. I don't really know what it is like to feel pressure when you are highly liked. The only admiration I get is a sad glance in the hallway every so often as if to say I pity his parents.

I'd be surprised how much a pep talk could change the temperament of everybody on the team. Perhaps if you try to share the burden with a couple of teammates, things will work out differently.

. . .

I'd really like to take the chance to say counselors can be invaluable folks. No need to be skeptical about stepping foot in one of their offices. Everything is done in strict confidence and respect. I doubt your position in school will affect whether they should or should not meet you for a session. I'm going to take a leap of faith here and please don't hate me for it, but I'm going to put your name down on a piece of paper and slide it under one of the counselor's doors.

Trust me on this, I'm not walking you into an ambush or anything. Except, I think there is more than what meets the eye. I can't seem to connect with you on that level, and it seems something is hurting. I never mentioned it until now, but I just want you to know I am aware of it, but I'm not exactly sure what it is, and how I should go about it. Nobody will know that you are going.

At either morning or afternoon registration, you will receive a letter slip, and that will outline your appointment. Please don't hate me for this, but I just want you to be happy. It seems like there's a sadness in your words occasionally that I don't know how to help you with. Plus, if you don't hate me after this, I'm still here to listen and try and talk about things if you desperately want. It's nice to know I cheer you up. My ramblings only work for so long, although, if I can be of assistance, I just want to help.

I've never known Justin Blake in such a manner before. I spend my time focused on my studies while in school, whereas you might have the chance to notice his facial expressions and hand gestures and whatnot... which might I add is weird. How is it you have come to see all these things about Justin. I don't tend to study a person's hand gestures or facial expressions and get to know what they like unless I like... *Oh... Em...Right...* weird question, but do you like Justin?

I KNOW I don't have the right to ask, but you've talked about him regularly in our messages, and I don't know why I did not see it sooner. You can tell me that I'm totally wrong here... and that I have gotten things backward.

However, before you do, I have nothing against folks who are different... or *gay* or... or... *sorry*. I don't mean for this to be awkward, but it's really okay if you are. I have a cousin in Phoenix whose gay and I'm happy for him. If you want to tell me it's your business, then, I'm sorry for prying, and I should've kept my mouth shut and pretended it wasn't there. I promise I won't tell anyone, I just want to be helpful, and you seem lost. Just to state the obvious, I like tacos... oh and Hershey's.

MY GOD, you are turning into me... your statement about feeling like you're drowning in your hobby is all too real an experience that I can relate to. If I didn't step away I'd go insane, so mind your mental health. If you take care of your juicy brain, your brain will take care of you. Be that as it may, I ponder every choice I make carefully in consideration before allowing myself to run with it.

The previous lines you have no idea how hard it was for me to confront you on the topic of sexuality. Again, I am deeply sorry if I have offended you on that, it's just I've done nothing more than praise my cousin, and I just wanted you to know that I am okay with it if you are.

. . .

When you are naturally adapt to a particular situation, you'll never understand what it is like to have it until it's gone. The mad world we live in is so crazy that you and I; we both have secrets about one another. Except, I just want to hold my secret back a little while longer. I'll get around to it. I promise just I don't have the phrases and words.

I don't want you to think less of me. Not many people talk to me because they think I'm helpless if I'm honest. You're the only friend I have... I don't have any other friends. I don't talk to anybody else outside school or in school. I am my own island, and I appreciate it in a way, only sometimes it does get lonely. I believe you'd make a great company as a friend, but with my secret, I don't want to disappoint you or feel ashamed. I'm not ready to meet you.

I just can't, not yet, I promise it's not about the contents of these letters, it is a personal problem. You never know what you have until it's gone, so treasure what you do have.

Please... I'll never forget this moment. I've gotten to talk to one of the most popular kids in the school, and the thing is he's really cool. I've learned a lot of things that I thought at first would have been hearsay. Though Max, you have bewildered me in a way I never knew possible. I love how you like classical music, not many kids our age do. I like it when you're openly honest. You have shared a great deal about your life, and I know I am not much of what you could consider somebody in your peer group, but I am impressed. I'm not trying to be closed-minded here although I never thought jocks could be as exciting as you. All we need to do now is show who we really are, and once we get past that hurdle, there will be no stopping us. Since I met you I've begun to talk to more people every day in school, I have affirmed that my education is not everything, that I should focus on my passions for the sake of enjoying them rather than excelling in them. If you think you haven't taught me much, then I think you have to guess again, you've shown me so much more. Plus, nothing's wrong if you're from Alabama... just saying.

PLUS, you should totally hang out with your little brother. If I had one, I would, even if they annoyed the crap out of me. Perhaps that is what you need. To let bygones be bygones so you can overcome the idea of you hating your brother. I repeat this is not an affiliate saying it is okay to bury your brother. I'm kidding, anyway I think I should call it here, I have said a lot of stuff that gives you lots to think about. I hope this doesn't make things between you and me awkward.

UNTIL NEXT TIME,
    Sherlock

ENTRY #19

To Sherlock,

I'M NOT sure what I am meant to say to your last letter... Look I'm *not* gay okay. It's not my fault I notice the little things other people do. Don't... I'm okay. To be clear, I'm not gay. I'm *not*.

You don't ask a person how to do things; you just notice them if you look for them. It's sick, I know. I've tried everything to make the thoughts stop. Except, every time I try, they never go away. They are in the back of my head like crickets on a warm night in July. You can't do anything about it. All I can do is listen to the humming. No matter how hard I try to stop the buzzing inside my brain, it *never* goes away. I'm not gay.

You can't tell anyone, okay. Please don't tell a soul. I want it to go away. I even think about if I can't make it leave. I assume that if I disappear, maybe, then I wouldn't have to deal with it. I didn't want to be this way. Why would God be so cruel, I've never done anything to deserve this. It makes me feel ugly, like a freak locked in a cage in a circus or a steaming pile of dog shit.

WHEN I WAS YOUNGER, I held the impression I could rid myself of my feelings. I even got sick thinking about it. I tried everything to make the horrible feeling that I was welcoming about my friends to go away. I tried scrubbing my junk with a scouring pad to stop me getting erections. Instead, I ended up at the hospital, but the thing that made me this way was still inside me. I don't want to be this way. I just want to be normal. I want to be able to like girls, tell them how pretty they are, kiss them, have sex with them, start a family, and have kids. Though, I can't, I don't feel anything towards girls. I don't know how to fix myself.

Sometimes I feel like I can't breathe, suffocating, and I can't tell anyone. I don't want to tell anyone, it makes me ill. Only, when I see Justin, it makes me wish I could be like that. How does he do it? How can the guy be so happy, fearless, and confident without feeling sick? I think the reason my dad treats me coldly is that deep down he might know. I don't want to be one of those kids on the street who is pointed at being called a faggot.

Last summer, I had my first girlfriend. Do you know Zoe on the cheerleading squad? Well, we were a thing for a while. Anyway, until Zoe figured something wasn't right. I wasn't trying to blow her off or anything, and I did work really hard to make myself like her.

I wasn't doing it to make my dad happy or my friends, I was attempting to prove to myself to like it. I wanted to be a standup guy. I walked her to school, carried her backpack, opened every door for her, made her smile and laugh, but now when I think about it, I was never smiling. I think things went a little sour when Zoe and I had our first kiss.

Every Fourth of July, my family throws a huge barbecue party in our backyard. All night I was trying to gather up the courage to kiss her. I won't lie. I was nervous, and I did genuinely want to kiss her. Except, something always held me back, I couldn't bring myself to do it, and that is until it was almost home time, and I walked her out onto my front porch.

While we waited for her mother to drop by, we sat on the porch swing and talked a little. It was then I got the impression Zoe knew I wanted to kiss her, and she wanted me to kiss her. In all of the craziest moments, I could come up with I decided to just go for it.

I turned to face her and said, "all right, I'll just go for it."

There it was, my first kiss in the entire world, and it wasn't as bad as I expected it to be, but I didn't feel anything. Zoe got all bashful, and when her mother arrived, she practically fell down the steps of the porch and climbed into the front seat of her mom's SUV.

A month later, Zoe and I were alone in her house since her parents had to attend some charity function. Therefore, I decided I'd stay at her place until her folks got back. I didn't have any malice intentions, though Zoe hinted toward me that she wanted to go further with our relationship.

Most boys would be thrilled by the prospect of having sex, but I couldn't enjoy it. I didn't want to be humiliated for not being able to do it; so all throughout the act, I thought of boys... I imagined Zoe was another guy while she gave me a blowjob until it happened.

Except, I don't think it fooled Zoe. She could sense

something was off, she even asked me a couple times when we were doing it.

The question was always, "do *you* like it?"

Can you imagine if she said to her girl-friends that I wasn't good at sex, that would be so bad? So, I had to try. After the night, Zoe did you know... She broke up with me one week later.

In a way, I was glad. Except, in another way, I wasn't because more girls were interested. When she gave the offer at first, I thought maybe this could be it, maybe Zoe can change me back. It seemed to take a lot longer than it ought to do. After the moment, I started to realize that maybe I'm never going to change. It's like I'm someone different every time I meet a new person. I'm starting to forget what identity I have created when I bump into these other people. I think it's gotten to a point, I don't even know who Max is anymore. One reason why I thought Alaska would be a cool place to go is that I can live out there and nobody will ever know me. My dirty secret and I will be hidden away forever, and I'll never have to share it with anyone.

EXCEPT, I've shared a lot of secrets with you now. I don't know what makes you so easy to talk to, but it feels good getting this off my chest. Please... Don't tell anyone... It will ruin me.

I'M sorry this letter is not long. Besides, I don't really have anything worth saying. I am eager to receive your message, that is if you don't decide to think I'm sick or something. Perhaps I am sick... or... Yeah...

. . .

Later,
   Watson

ENTRY #20

To Watson,

RELAX OKAY, I'm not going to tell anybody. I mean, I can't believe I'm right. Usually, I am the type of person to excel academically, but miss the par when it comes to humans. I promise my lips are sealed and nobody will know what we have talked about. I don't identify with how it feels to be gay, or what I should say to try and make things better. Except, I am inclined to say there is nothing wrong with you. You are just sailing in an entirely different vessel compared to my identity. Are you sure it's not a phase? I don't... I hope this does not sound corny or offensive or anything. How do you know it's not a phase? I hear some people can experience short spans in their lifetimes when something happens to be true, then there comes a day when all the truth in that matter turns to dust. Soon what once was turns to speckles in the past and all that is left is little squiggles floating in the air. First, I'm going to say something incredibly corny... you're not sick. You are just abnormal; like wonderfully normal like the abominable snowman which is incredibly abnormal, but beautifully normal.

I'M KIDDING, of course, you are still the awesome person I got to know. So, I don't think whether you're gay, bisexual, pansexual, asexual, demi-sexual, biromantic, Klingon-sexual or Ulysses himself then I don't care. All I care about is the person I've been talking to, not the label attached. If it's any recollection to ease your mind, I'm straight... there everything is out in the open now. As long as you don't start calling me bruh, I think we should be fine.

I think a deep part of you is trying to tell yourself that you are what you are, and there is no changing it. You must first learn to love at home, that home being yourself, must come first before you can begin to accept the idea for others. I just want to say even with the news, nothing will ever change between us. Well, I hope not, you are still the fastest runner I know in school and a pretty talented guy.

I have seen you playing football before, and you are pretty quick. Except, I understand why you want to put the lacrosse down for a while along with football. I suppose you probably had that dream to be one day on the Super Bowl, playing on a field and adored by millions. Just, the only person you should seek validation from is yourself, the rest will follow. Perhaps try not to overwork your brain anymore and stop cooking it on high heat.

Let things be, and I'm assuming things will begin to work out. I think there's enough material in your life for your very own TV melodrama... I'm teasing, of course. Nonetheless, who could have predicted the life of a popular high school student could be so complicated and diverse. From the way you describe it seems you have been protecting this particular part of yourself for so long that you almost wish it weren't true.

I RECKON my conclusion about the only other gay kid in school is correct. You do to have a crush on that boy, perhaps when things begin to turn in your favor, and you're more comfortable with yourself, maybe you can work up to asking him out. Yeah, I can see how you mean it is weird to talk about another guy like this.

You know, whatever it is you have to do to ask the guy out, you should definitely ask him out if you fancy him or someone you do like, I mean. I'm sorry, I'm jumping to conclusions. You see I've never had a gay friend before so it's like totally cool to have one and, I don't know it's like I want to be a fountain of knowledge for my gay compadre. No idea why I am talking like this now.

AS FAR AS Zoe on the cheerleading squad goes... no. Perhaps it is highly likely for you to know the girls who sing and flaunt to a crowd before every game, but I just look at the girls. I do not fit into any social circle, nor do I have the luxury to be in the company of pretty girls. Sometimes I do become preoccupied looking at the girls to understand what their names are.

I reckon at times, I am a little absent-minded in that regard as I am a nerd of sorts. I guess I am the guy who drools when he sees a hot chick in denim shorts and a plaid shirt. Just to put it out there for the future. I hope you can trust me enough to feel like you can tell me anything. I won't judge. I think you are awesome.

Okay. Plus, if there is something you wish to know about me, don't be afraid to ask. I am open to discussion.

Anyway, I better go, I'll catch up with you at a later time.

Until next time,
  Sherlock

ENTRY #21

To Sherlock,

Hey, I know I picked a shitty time to come out I guess. I can't remember what I wrote in the last letter, all I can recall is that I kept saying that I'm not. Man, it felt like the longest weekend in my entire life waiting for a reply from you. I figure I do have a knack for choosing the right time. Thank you. Thank you for not bailing on me or thinking I'm sick. You know the first thing when I came into school this morning, I was greeted to a fight between a couple in the corridor outside my homeroom.

Typically, I'd be the type of person to break the fight up, but not today. It's hard to explain what I've been feeling for so long that anytime I try to think about it, it's numb. I had a lot of time to myself on Saturday and Sunday, and all I thought about was I hope I don't lose the only real friend I have. From the start, you have been nothing but kind to me, and I'm incredibly grateful for that.

If you have ever been bullied by people I know, or

maybe me, I'm so sorry. I never thought about the repercussions of saying what I said in the letter could be used for blackmail. Except, I'm trusting you are a more stand-up guy than me so I won't mention any more about the matter. Hell, I took your advice, and I didn't wait for you to go to a counselor. I have an appointment for Wednesday, so I'm going to see the school therapist so to speak.

Legitimately I could barely crawl out of bed this morning, but when I got to the homeroom, and I checked the mailbox, you have no idea how I felt. It was like I could exhale when I saw your overwhelming sense of acceptance within the first paragraph. I started to tear up in class. By the time I got to the end of the letter, the shortest we have had in a long time might I add, a sense of joy had overcome me. It didn't feel like I was juggling the Empire State building on one shoulder and the Burj Khalifa on the other. It was like this blanket of shame was lifted, and I feel happy now, but at the same time, I'm still a little sad, but not depressingly sad.

I think I have been battling with myself for a number of years. I can't believe I'm saying all of these things so easily when not only it's hard to admit to myself, but you also know who I am. I guess all along I just wanted someone to understand, and you do… ish. I don't quite understand what it means to be normal, only it seems as if I can breathe easily for now. The rest of my life is still a blur, but I presume I will get by.

You are right, I am hard on *myself*. Do you think anyone else would know by looking at me? Would you know if you didn't know me? Sorry, I'm just rooting for assurance. What makes us so analytical concerning ourselves? Why is it I seek validation from pinpointing out every flaw I have rather than trying to embrace it and adapt to make it work for me? Anytime I chase my insecurities it's like I'm hunting myself with a machete in hand.

The only thing I'm doing is carving out a more horrible presumption of who I honestly am. I'm not trying to be self-assured here, but I think I'm an okay person. I mean, I'm not stupid, and I'm good at a lot of things. I don't deliberately hurt, not unless I am trying to defend myself. So, why is it, it only takes one molecule or a problem to drown out the effects of many great.

I'm nervous about going to the counselor on Wednesday. I've never talked to anyone about my emotions before. Does it make me pathetic? Perhaps does it make me look weak? Will I have to talk about my sexuality to them?

I apologize, I'm fishing for answers, again aren't I? It's just... nevermind. I'll play it out and see how it goes. Yeah, I'll just be brave about the whole situation. Why does it feel like I'm going for a major operation or something? The anticipation is not what I expected it to be... God these last few letters really do leave a lasting impression on my so-called mental stability. I promise, I'm A-OK, and I repeat not, I'm not going to jump off a building or sink myself to the bottom of the nearest bay.

On Saturday I was looking over the old letters you wrote to me. I hope it's not weird, but I kept all your messages. They are safe inside a drawer of my desk in my bedroom. I read all the things you sent to me while I was waiting out the anticipation of what was to come today... Monday.

We were like so random and funny.

Now things are like serious... talk about a buzz kill. I have a habit of killing the positive energy in the room, huh?

I have noticed other guys in a couple different grades who might be gay, but the only person I know in our year... well, my year is him. I guess you could say I have a little crush... oh man, I'm cringing writing this, but I do fancy him just a little bit.

I find I have nothing else to say. I can't lie about it, though I just feel like sharing. You know so much about me, and I don't know anything about you. The only thing I do know is that you play an instrument, you like science, you're smart, thoughtful, and funny. Everything else is a blur, I don't know who my best friend is. My other best friend, sure he's there for me, but not for something like this. Would it be wrong to say or even suggest that I like you more? I mean, I have no secrets left. You know every aspect of my life now, and I don't know anything about you, nothing. Can you tell me something about you, something real, something Sherlock?

Anyway, I have to get going to class, you know to be the normal kid everyone wants me to be.

LATER,
　　Max

ENTRY #22

To Max - aka Watson,

I SEE you've changed your alias; a pseudonym is getting old. Unfortunately, I'm not ready to share certain aspects of my life, but I suppose my name is relatively common. So, I reckon I can give you my name. I hope this doesn't give away too much information and make you think less of me for being the way I am, and since I have conducted some research, I have concluded that there are approximately 27 people in our school with the name Isaac, eight within our two grades.

Therefore, perhaps I will be one of those eight you will encounter now in your day-to-day life. I won't approach you, I'm not that sort of person, remember. I'm the Brainiac, I like the puzzles. Maybe if you follow the cheese, I'll leave a trail and possibly you'll find the real Isaac. I can already sense it in my bones; the twinge of panic and excitement. I will rise to my feet and go berserk with crippling nervousness and skedaddle if you look my direction. The real question is how many Isaac's do you know?

A clue is a clue, make use of it because I like having you around. Only, most of my life, I have been navigating away from attachment because people feel sorry for me, they always do. Sometimes I don't want them to.

I am flattered that you think of me that way, friends are hard to come by, many come and go. Who would have thought I'd befriend another guy who is on the other side of the fence as I. Your popular, I'm not, but it goes to show that barriers don't need to exist. We've managed by ourselves, and I am glad that I signed up for the assignment. If you want to know something true about me; the reason I put my name down for the pen pal collaboration is that I am lonely. My mom is suffocating, and I know she tries her best, and I love her, but I don't go outside too much, I don't make friends easy.

So just once in my life, I needed to talk to someone. When I heard that I didn't need to give my identity, I thought I could be whoever I aspired to be to get the other person to like me on the other side of the letters. Only, I never felt like I was obliged to do that, you just made me your friend. I have never felt more accepted than I did before then; than I do now. Having a place to belong is gratifying, so I like you back, for taking the time to listen to me.

I was so sure that if people knew it was me, they'd ask for another partner. Oh, boy was I wrong. I am glad I was.

YOU AND I can agree on one thing for sure, shame, guilt, and hoping for more seems to be a way of life. Does it ever live up to something worthwhile? You see a couple of years ago, things changed for me, and my life has never been the same.

I am confident, insecurities at least, should not be the source of all your troubles. Some people have significant complexities. I am one of them. I'm certainly not much of a story so to speak. My life is pretty dull compared to what it ought to be. People change, just like me.

I WILL NOT BLACKMAIL YOU, you have my sincerity in the matter. I have been punished enough to understand that you should never kick another person in the gut while they are at their lowest or most vulnerable.

MAX, you make a great companion, you have been open and frank with me. I know I haven't been explicitly clear with my background. Naturally, I retain little material to tell other than subjects within science, movies, and music.

It might sound depressing, it may seem lonely, or you could say I might not be expanding my horizons. However, to me, those are the worlds I live in, and they have kept me here. Witnessing magic unfold in front of your eyes is the greatest gift I know.

Humans are a collection of energy; when we put this power to work for good intentions, passion, and validation only then do we discover the actual benefits of being alive. It is the simple things we regretfully rebuke; they tied us together. The smile one gives when passing another on a sidewalk walking their dog. How one holds the door open to be pleasant; the other party runs to show gratitude.

When we hear goosebump music, we understand without having to open our mouths. People automatically realize the power of this energy, and that's what makes a home. Sometimes the missing feeling inside your chest is not that something is missing, but that you lack contentment. A home begins when you grasp the concept of what it is you wish to place in the home. I'd love to have a home built strictly out of chocolate and have a constant milkshake stream run through the living room. Except that would be a house and not a home.

I use the word home, not in the context you might imagine, but when you think about it, all that energy inside of you has a home and making that home colorful and beautifully gay is what you need to do. I say embrace what it is you feel and don't ever underestimate the urge to cry, be confused with yourself or to just run as you have never run before. *Don't* be so hard on yourself. It's good to hear that the weight of the Burj Khalifa and the Empire State has been lifted... I have a question... But how many years of weight training did it take you to raise those buildings? I want in on that superhuman strength.

You are strong; you'll work things out, I just know you will. You seem like the type of person, that when you have a plan, and you know where it is you want to go, you'll go.

I KNOW I beat myself up consistently, but nothing ever stops me from getting out of bed in the morning. I have my troubles sure, and that's a part of me, but I think the real reason I get out of bed each day is to come to school, to see people, to see life.

Oddly, it makes me fortunate to see others happy, even if I am furious on the inside. So, just relax for the first time in forever; and you'll ace the counselor session on Wednesday.

ANYWAY, I got to go, my mom sent me a message telling me

she is here to pick me up. It's after school hours, but I needed to stay back to do some assignments. That's the lie I told my mom. The real reason is, I just desired to sit in a room to clear my head. Anything beats the world outside my bedroom, but getting to write to you has made the silent endurance so much more comforting.

Until next time,
  Isaac

ENTRY #23

To Isaac,

Wow, what a dick move; I'm kidding, of course. I'm smiling at the letter right now while I am writing this and it's weird comprehending that you have a name other than Sherlock. Not to be mean or anything, although I didn't think you'd have a name like Isaac. Isaac is a nice name. I don't know what I must have been expecting.

However, I have this warm sensation in my chest, and it makes me feel like I recognize you a whole lot better now that I know your name. I have no reason not to trust you, and you have been very forthcoming with me. Therefore, your word is held in high regard. Though dude... Your piece about approximately how many Issacs's reside in the building, now that is pure genius.

I must inquire what cheese you are indicating. Are we talking about smelly cheese? Perhaps yummy cheese? Cheese crumbs? Cheese Streaks? Cheese gone wild! Ah... I amuse myself sometimes.

. . .

You know I have already bumped into two Issacs this morning. That's what you want, right? You want me to find you actively. I didn't approach any Issacs I am not acquainted with; however, I don't think they were you. Is it weird to presume I can tell that just by looking at them? I still have six people to go, and typically I am confident and energetic about going into such matters.

Except, I'm nervous. I'm afraid the only real friend I have ever made will think less of me, or something will get muddled when we meet. I hope I honestly didn't do anything in the past to hurt you. I know I have been uncool about some of my altercations in school. I just hope of all things I'm not proud of, that you're not one of them. I'll follow your trail.

Only you're going to have to leave some more clues other than your name. I'm still going to look for you actively.

So far, I know a guy called Isaac who does art, he is majorly popular among his peer groups, but not the entire school. The other is a loner, he keeps to himself. I overheard some people saying that the guy is called Isaac. I learned this guy likes to spend his evenings after school in the library. Except I have a good feeling that it's not you either. Maybe I'm wrong, I don't know, but am I getting closer. What will it be like if we finally meet? Will we just continue where we left off in our letters, or do we start all over again? I'm like super hyped to try and locate you. I know, I know, I'll just be patient, and things will finally work its way around.

I have a horrible habit digging for answers to questions I don't even know are there in the first place. I want to be a good friend, I need someone who understands, and you understand.

I'M glad that you did not reject my praise. Friends are hard to come by, and I guess one reason why I don't want to lose you is... well... you are hard to come by. A rare find indeed. I know, right... if the two of us were only starting up again and we had dropped a line about where we are now, I'd probably laugh or at least snigger.

We really are getting on well, barriers never existed between you and I. We just talked to one another, from revealing everything, it all became a possibility.

YOU KNOW, all this time you have been helping me with my problems, and now that I hear some things you are dealing with, it's like I don't know what to say. In a way, it is empowering and gratifying to grasp and realize that you have shared a part of yourself with me after all this time. I'm not as fancy with words as you might be, though I won't suffocate you or constantly annoy you.

I reckon I'd be the type of person to drop by unannounced and take you swimming for the day. After all, you did mention you love to swim. I'll make you a deal, if I can figure out who you are by Saturday, you have to take me swimming. If I don't figure out who you are by Saturday, I promise to teach you how to play lacrosse or something. If I lose, after school, you can turn up to the playing field behind the building. If I win, you meet me at the aquatic center across from Griffith Park. Deal?

. . .

I KNOW FOR A FACT, I don't want to live my life anymore in the dark. Isaac, you have made me want to be a better person, and I don't know how to thank you for helping me come to that realization. I have come to learn that: through you, life is what you make of it. You seem to have a wisdom that I've never encountered before from another person. It's like you sometimes speak of another time. And you always linger on a moment in time, where you seem to be teaching me to savor what I have because I won't understand unless it's gone. This all brings me to some preposterous notion that something might have happened in your past. I just wanted you to know: you have been incredible to me. I really need you to know that whatever it is you have gone through in the past, and still deal with, it is not going to make any difference as to why I still wish to talk to you. I get it now. When I first started chatting, I always knew something was up. I never imagined that it could be as big as it appears now. Though I don't know what it entails, I'm still going to look for you, and if you decide that you want to share that aspect of your life with me, I'm here.

CRAZY TO BELIEVE we are practically like the same person. It's not until you quote something the way you do that stuff naturally piece together. The way you word sentences and the little mundane day-to-day quests we all have to embark on, makes' living in this world substantially better when you describe them the way you do. I didn't think I'd be open or persuaded to believe that we are all systematically connected to one another to this energy you speak of. How you described it makes me feel appreciative of these little moments in time. The next time I am out, and someone's walking the dog, and they smile at me, I'll appreciate that more than I have in the past.

In an odd way, you have persuaded me that there is an excellent underlying value to most things' humans do. Even if it gets muddled along the way, it's what we do with the subject that counts. Sometimes, Isaac, you freak me out.

If I had any knowledge, I'd presume you were living inside my head. I assume you have experienced the hole that seems to throb inside your chest from time to time when you don't know what your purpose is.

However, I've come to realize that you are right... there is no purpose, just contentment for what you want to do. If you are at war with yourself, then you can never be content. For as long as I can remember, it's like I have been trying to find what is supposed to fit into the numbness inside my chest.

Yet, I woke up this morning feeling refreshed, like I had been given an alternative path to venture. It's all thanks to you. I don't know where I got my superhuman strength from, but I have come to recognize having struggles defines who you are. I guess without all these little hiccups and pop-ups in life there would be nothing worth mentioning. That is our story, and without it, it wouldn't be exciting.

I'm not an analytical person, however, I am eager, and I pursue and act when I believe it needs to be taken. Asking you out; not in the traditional fashion, but to get you out of your comfort zone, I am willing to try just that.

. . .

Later,
　　Max

ENTRY #24

To Max,

I KNOW WHAT YOU MEAN; my name does have a ring to it, doesn't it? Thanks. Max is a nice name too, but I totally agree my name is better.

I know, right... It's savage. It took me the best part of three days to figure out how many others were in our school. I was planning to tell you for a couple of days now, though you actually asked me. You beat me to it.

In correlation with my hints, it most definitely has to be cheese gone wild! I'll admit, I got a chuckle out of that. I know we've gone completely against the rules, and I'm not typically one to break a system that has been set down. Besides, since we are near the end of the projected assignment, I suppose it's adequately put to know each other's names now.

It makes me wonder if anyone else from our project knows each other's names or if we are the only ones. It's hard to imagine how both of us began knowing nothing regarding one another, and now we know a lot about each other.

It has been time well spent, all the free time I mean in school writing to you. I had no inkling that such small-time merit could turn into a desire. I reckon that's how I feel on any given day. I believe you said it in our previous letters, and I'm stating it now. Turning up to see that you have written to me makes my day.

JUST WITH THE possibility of finally meeting you coming to a close, I'm apprehensive too. At the start, I wasn't sure whether our conversations would take up off the ground, yet here we are. I think we've gotten to the point that we've discussed everything deserving a question, and only our day-to-day necessities are worth asking for. Well that's the way I see it, I know there is more to talk about, but I feel like that is best done in person.

I DON'T MEAN to be a buzzkill, then what you said about actively finding me is weirdly humbling and scary. I have the one and only Max Wilson trying to guess who I am. Now that I am even more aware and alert to the plausibility of our meeting, it's like I don't want our letters to end.

I'm not an artist, I can't even draw a circle, let alone a stick-man. The guy in the library sounds like a preferable candidate, sadly I don't spend much time reading books in the school library. I tend to go to the local branch because they have real science books. Our school facilities don't have any attractive content to stimulate my brain. I assume in a way and don't judge, our school caters for those who can handle a less capable knowledge.

In a way, they stock media that will be of a typical easiness for students to absorb. Hence, I look elsewhere for material to regurgitate. Although I did see you today... I'm not going to lie about that. I saw you enter the library, so you must be doing the leg work detective. It didn't register with me then until I read your letter now that you are inherently looking for me, like really. I thought it was just in our conversations at first, but wow, it's inspiring to be admired for a change. Therefore, a hint can be as follows; the library is not a place I go, but I occasionally roll past the fine establishment on my way to class. Now whatever way class is, I'll let you try to make heads or tails of this on your own.

I'M GOING to be brazened here, this weekend you're playing a match, right? I'll turn up with the audience, of course. However, I'm going to make a dare since you have called me out in your previous letter. I'd like nothing more than to learn how to play lacrosse or go swimming with a friend who is not my little cousin. I just want to see if you are genuine. I have a history of these sorts of things. So, for another hint when you're out on the field just after the national anthem, I dare you to snatch the microphone from whoever is singing afterward, and yell into the mic, "*the cheese has gone wild.*"

I DON'T KNOW something about upping the stakes seems devious and honestly, I like it. I don't have a lot left to hint; once you catch on, I think you'll understand. If you do this, I promise I'll give you another clue, a big clue. There is nothing more eye-opening than a person who is willing to make a fool of themselves for friendship. Plus, I'll repay the debt once you figure out who I am, I'll do something stupid too, purely for amusement.

I HAD *NOTHING* TO REJECT, therefore, what would I decline. Incredibly sweet of you to say, I don't quite know what to say to that. Thanks. A couple of weeks ago, I presumed if we'd known each other, however, never spoke to one another, I'd reckon we'd have passed each other in the hallways without a second thought.

Except, I don't want to take credit for something I didn't do. I surmise I was in the right place at the correct time. Just all the work you have made is simply you. I've had no hand in helping you realize anything. Perhaps I helped remove the wool over your eyes. You've done the same for me. So, for the sake of thanking one another, lets just put it out there that we both appreciate each other's efforts.

MIND YOU, I will hold you to the promises you keep. Therefore, be sure to commit upon inciting them. So, yeah, besides science, swimming is my escape. Just like music is yours. I love to swim. At the moment I'm toning my biceps. When I finish every girl will be looking at me; not anymore will I be that skinny kid who is apparently there, yet never paid attention toward.

Your preposterous notion is correct, something happened in my past a couple of years ago. Four years ago, to be exact. Given that I'm almost 15, I had turned 11 two weeks earlier before my life changed. It made me appreciate life even more afterward. Can you imagine, I'm not lying. I was dead for 15 minutes.

Really sums up how the small insignificant things don't

seem to matter anymore after you've had a life-changing ordeal. Perhaps I've ruined the surprise. Perhaps... maybe I've given too much away. Admittedly, there can only be one Isaac with a history like mine.

I HAVE another thing to confess that I never told you before. Actually, I lied. See my mom's dead... and I'm in a *wheelchair*. I'm the *cripple*, everyone sees, *pities*, but never *includes*.

SHIT... so much for following the cheese. Sorry for lying Max. I just... I wanted to feel normal. Except, I didn't lie about everything else. I really do swim. Plus, I do play an instrument, and I do like science. As I said, I'm toning my biceps.

ANYWAY, I think I will call it here, and it's been cool, you know. I understand if you don't want to hang around with someone like me. I'll just hold you back from doing all the fun shit.

UNTIL NEXT TIME, or goodbye,
    Isaac

ENTRY #25

To Isaac,

OH, YOU. I mean, I know who you are now. I'm sorry about your condition, I figure that sucks. Em... yeah, everything kind of make sense now. I am a little agitated that you lied, but I can see why you might have wanted to hide your situation. In a way, I am sorry for having kept talking about being able to run all over the place, and teaching you how to play sports or I don't know, like... being lazy. You said you swim, except how do you do that if you are in a wheelchair. Plus, being in a wheelchair all the time, does that mean you can't feel anything south of your hips. Em... does that mean everything below is... not working. Sorry for asking, I'm just... I feel weird grasping what I know now.

IT'S AWKWARD YOU KNOW, realizing how I have been talking smack all this time about being energetic and well, being able to walk just about anywhere I want. You kept dropping hints all along, about having something taken away that I wouldn't be able to understand, until it's gone, and I presume I'll never perceive what it is like to lose my independence.

Em, Isaac, it might be wrong for me to say this. Though I'm pretty sure it won't work: us being friends. You live a different life, a complicated one, and well, I live another. I don't care about your disability, per se.

What I really mean is... I don't think I can be friends with you because I have special feelings, regardless of what way you present yourself. Can I be in *love* with someone and not care about how they look. I'm serious, this is odd and weird. All I know is that I have a strong ripely sensation in my stomach, and it makes me feel ashamed to acknowledge who you are and still like you. I mean, what if I desired to do wild things with you, like rock climbing, how do we do that? Actually, how do you swim, do you need someone to help you all the time or can you do that yourself.

I RECKON you are right about your previous statement; that neither of us would have talked to each other if it were not for these letters. I'll be honest, okay, not that I have anything against you or people in your position. Just, I don't think I can deal with something this heavy. I have enough things on my mind, and I don't want to worry extra about you when you can't keep up with my friends or me if I was to invite you out. I... I em... I... You know, it kind of sucks you know... that you are in a wheelchair if I am honest.

Somehow, I always imagined if we got together, we'd be able to do wild shit, and well I don't know what I was thinking making a preconceived notion that you could just walk based on my own knowledge. Except, now that I know

I just feel guilty for being nice to you now that I know about you. I am thankful I never made fun of you, and that I never ridiculed somebody in your situation.

Only, it seems like such a shitty thing to do to such a nice person. Whenever I saw you in the corridor at school, I always assumed or asked myself at least, "what did that guy do to piss off god?"

THOUGH NOW THAT I know you are a phenomenal person beneath the appearance it makes me hate myself for not reaching out sooner or at least trying when I knew for a fact that you seemed lonely and lost in your everyday life when I'd see you.

I think I have been too caught up in my own life to genuinely care about anyone else, and since I met you, you have opened me up to the plausibility of being open to people.

Is it wrong for me to wish the accident happened to me, rather than a grateful person like you? What I really want to say is that I can't be just a friend, and now that I know it's you, it makes me want to be helpful, yet, honestly, these uncharted waters petrify me.

CAN I ask what really happened? How did it really happen? And I'm really sorry about your mom. Mom's are so much better than dad; even though I love my dad... Mom always knows. I'm super sorry about what occurred, four years ago.

Did you see the other side? I mean, heaven.

Your superhuman Isaac... you know that. All this time,

I've been passing by a superhero on my way to class for the last couple of years. After what you have gone through I can appreciate why you savor the little things now that they don't seem significant when you have them to dispose of.

Plus, please don't call yourself a cripple, nobody calls you that. I didn't even know your name... I always referred to you as the kid in the wheelchair. Yes, you are the only person in the entire school, I have noticed who has a wheelchair. I understand it is not the best way to refer to someone, on just what I see, though you are totally worth the time and effort, in getting to know.

Lastly, it will never be goodbye with me. You have made it into my inner circle of besties. I'm dealing with stuff, so sorry if I am slow on the uptake, but I just need some time to think that's all. I'll let you know... you know when things are clear. I just, I wasn't expecting my best friend to be in a wheelchair. Though you are still alright in my books...

Until next time,
   Max

ENTRY #26

To Max,

I GET IT, it's uncanny, you didn't expect me to be sitting in a wheelchair, and I know it is a crappy thing to have done to you. I don't like lying, it isn't me as a person. It makes me extremely guilty when I stop to ponder how it must be to be when you have been forthcoming and overwhelmingly positive since the get-go. I should have just been transparent with the topic, as you have been with me. Furthermore, it is okay about the physical activity aspect, I never took any heed to it, and well... you could have never known anyway, so, what is the point of getting angry about this.

To your questions, I swim using my arms, I cannot explain the process, though, since you kind of float in water, it makes it easier for me to do that as a past time. I played soccer before in the wheelchair with a support group I was a part of for a while, they used to get somebody to push the wheelchair, and I'd hold the ball on my lap as they pushed my chair.

My only regret is that I never got to try football. In a way, working as a team is rather exciting and also rewarding to do. Though no, I don't feel anything below my hips, well except... em, you know my junk... sometimes. It works, just when it wants to. Peeing is okay, but everything is messed up... ish.

I ASSUME I did drop a lot of hints about not doing stuff since we first started writing, and I understand why you probably don't want to talk to me anymore. I hope it is only temporarily, and we can go back to being friends, that is if you still crave to be. I had a feeling that if I did tell you that we'd stop being friends. It's not easy for someone to watch after me all the time, or to have the constant thought in your mind every minute.

I reckon it takes the joy out of the time, knowing you have to be responsible for a person who is semi-dependent. Only, I promise you, I can do a lot more than you think. I can do most things you can do, other than walk obviously. Just smaller things like climbing stairs take longer; for instance, I'd have to scooch my way gradually to the top of a staircase. Things take time, but I'm not entirely broken.

OH... em, I was just replying to what you were saying before I took the time to read your letter, and now that I have come to a particular paragraph I'm not sure what I should say about something you have written.

First off, I wish to say thank you for accepting me, or I'm not sure since I took the time out to read your entire letter now, and it says at the end of the message that you want to take time out.

If I am missing something, please tell me, but I don't want to lose you as a friend. If I could fix what happened to me, I would, but I can't. It occurred, and I ain't got the power to do those sorts of miracles.

EM, *love* is a strong word to say to someone you have never met. I like you to, but not that way, of course. Though this is hard, I know, but I'm not gay. I think things have changed between us and there may be an adjustment period, or perhaps we just were never meant to be. For now, all I can say is cool... although it's a little odd, I don't mind it.

I just don't want to lose what we have built up. Therefore, Max, I am incredibly touched. So, I guess I'll try and start again. Is it even worth beginning all over, or is it past that point? If not, hi, I'm Isaac, I'm 15-years old, I'm in 10th Grade, and not only am I in a wheelchair, but I am a science geek, and I kickass at swimming. Well 9th Grade, would you like to start again?

YOU KNOW, sometimes I ask the same question as I lay awake at night, searching for answers in the busy avenues of my brain. What did I do to him upstairs, to have to live like this? The answer is nothing; just a silence distills. God never responds. God is not there. He is a phony. As to how it happened, we were on the freeway, coming home on Monday afternoon from spending some time up at the lake house our family owns.

Dad left earlier as he took a week off from work and had to be back in the city. Dad drove home on Sunday evening, and mom and I followed on the next day as it was summer.

We drove a good two hours, and we got pretty close to the city.

Just, a few cars ahead, someone must have recently changed a flat tire, and never put the wheel back on correctly. Before mom could react, driving the vehicle, this projectile bounced off the windshield. Instantly, the glass cracked, the screen turned a milky white, and I couldn't see the road in front of us. Somehow mom got scared, she swerved to avoid the tire bobbing along. Only, it still hit us and well the car barrel-rolled, three times to be exact.

WE ENDED up on the other side of the highway.

THE BACKPACK I had between my legs with snacks and drinks in it, came from the floor well. I was sitting in the front seat, I remember the bag hitting my face as the car tumbled. It's like everything hurt for a moment, and I couldn't take control of anything. Plus, something happened with the daylight. It like stuttered, or flaked out.

You know like those old super 8 cameras; the way the light flickers inside. Then everything stopped, and it was calm for a moment. Lastly, I recall hearing a loud crash, and then I don't remember anything after that.

FOR THAT SPLIT SECOND when the car calmed down, I've never been as scared in all my life. I wish people never felt that way when it happens to them, thought the sad fact is it does occur. I woke two days later in the hospital, everyone thought it was a miracle I was alive.

They told me I *died* in the ambulance on the way to the

hospital. Though I felt different; I thought for a second, I was living outside my body, and then tried moving my arms, even though it was sore.

I then attempted to move my legs and realized they didn't work. I knew then I'd never walk again; the seatbelt impression left on my chest suggested it saved me. Though I later learned another car plowed into us from the front of the vehicle, and yet, my mom died. Dad takes care of me now, and he is overprotective.

The footwell squished and did its damage on my legs. I was supposedly bleeding really bad, and that's all they told me. They skipped the fact my mom died, even though I was asking for her all the time. They never told me where she was as soon as I came around. Then when dad told me, I went psycho, so much, they had to sedate me. So there... no more secrets. I'm Isaac Miller; once an adventurous kid, yet, still with a joyful heart.

Please just don't leave me hanging, okay. Even if you don't want to talk to me, just tell me. Besides, I'll turn up to watch you play this weekend. I won't miss that.

Eh... Later,
    Isaac

ENTRY #27

To Isaac,

Sorry, I have not spoken to you in a couple of days, and I swear it's not that you have caused me to be this way. It's just I was shocked a little, that's all. I'm not saying it's weird for you to be in the wheelchair. Actually, I guess it's cool... well, that's not exactly what I mean, when I phrase it like that. I repeat I am not saying your accident was cool. Ugh... I'm useless at expressing myself, aren't I? What I am trying to say is, well... I don't know what I am attempting to announce. What I want you to remember is that you and I are cool.

I know the questions I asked during your revelation might have bordered on intrusive. So, I apologize for asking in the first place. Secondly, who am I to judge, regardless if you are in a wheelchair. For a second, I'll be open about the subject. Though, for a moment, I was cynical about your condition. I went home that evening and reflected about it all night, and I just kept rerunning the day in my head. How

I sat down at the table and how I was not prepared to hear that you are paralyzed from the waist down.

RIGHT, that's not so good, about not being able to operate Moby Dick. Em... So... no hard feelings, right? And no that is not an innuendo. It's just one guy saying to another, I'm sorry that your dick doesn't work... or you know, just I feel bad.

Over the last couple of days, I have had some time to reflect, and well now that you have mentioned it in your letter, it makes me want to meet you even more now. Isaac, you seem like a fighter to me, and that is pretty awesome. I'm not sure how we'd play Lacrosse with a wheelchair, though I can certainly push you around if you want to play football. I'll get you to the end zone to score a touchdown.

Have you ever scored a goal when you were like really young with your dad or anything? Plus, I understand what you are on about, with swimming. Except, I get really tired when I just use my arms all the time and not my feet.

I'D BE DOWN to team up for sporting activities, that is if you wish to collaborate with me. I'd love to team up with you, of course. Yeah, now that I have begun to look over some of your older notes, I've come to notice a series of events, where you did pass on the required information. Only, as I have told you in the past, I'm not the brightest tool in the shed... I mean the sharpest tool in the shed.

Though I get-by. It's not that I don't want to talk to you, I totally do, and I am passed that phase right now. I'm good as new, and I'm sorry I stopped speaking to you for the last 2 days.

You said you are pretty independent, so why would I need to watch you like a babysitter. Even if we did get together, and I'd have to help you like up some stairs, I don't think that would be too large a task as to kill the fun.

I don't know how you can recall that amount of detail, and still be not sad about the situation. I mean, what you wrote has deeply affected me after I read about the car accident. I presume that is what they say about your life flashing before your eyes when something like this does happen. I know God might not be there all the time, though he does listen. Even if it doesn't always work, it's nice to have something to pray to, to ask advice.

Sometimes, there is not a lot of folks you can talk to about things, and well he was the first person I told about my sexuality. I prayed to be cured, although he never answered, I began to resent the way I am, and just continued on with my everyday life as if the problem wasn't there. Except, when I prayed, it was nice to have something to focus on rather than having nobody to believe in.

Sometimes life sucks, I get that. People do terrible things to each other. Though there is always hope at the end of the tunnel, in the form of light. When you reach those rays, I guess things are clearer for a person who has led and lived a terrible ordeal.

Now, with you wanting to fix yourself, well I guess the two of us would like to correct a lot of things. Sadly, that sort of wand does not exist, but only in books and movies. Sure, things have changed, though that doesn't mean, I like talking to you any less.

. . .

I suppose, being scared is a valuable asset when we are uncertain. The anxious sensation clopping around in our chest and stomach gives us the power to keep going, and in a way, it has made me realize that it is okay to be uncomfortable. I don't think I am as brave as you thought, Isaac. I cry and get upset over what people might think of me rather than appreciating that the only persons' opinion that should have some weight is mine and mine alone.

The only time I have ever been genuinely petrified was when I was about eleven, and I still had problems wetting the bed. I used to get up in the middle of the night, put my laundry in the washing machine, then the dryer and put it back on my bed before my mom would get up the next morning.

I asked her one day out of the blue, to show me how to work the machines because I was "just curious" as to how, and she did teach me. I lost many hours of sleep, I even looked like Frankenstein's monster. I was petrified of anyone ever finding out. I got things under control about a year later, though, it's still really embarrassing to know that I pee'd all over myself and could never wake up in the time to go to the bathroom. My mom doesn't know, well if she does, she has kept it quiet.

Therefore, I am concluding that my mother never found out about my 3AM adventures to the garage. Though she did ask my dad one morning during breakfast if he was doing extra laundry, that the detergent was running out more often without an explained reason. So, I started buying my own detergent with my pocket money, and hid the washing power in my bedroom, under my bed with all my childhood toys. You can imagine how embarrassing this is for a twelve-year-old.

You can picture my alarm when I came home one afternoon, and mom had pulled out all the stuff from beneath the bed to donate unwanted crap. Except, she questioned me about the detergent. I still don't know to this day how I managed to persuade her it was for a side project I picked up in school. For the next couple of months, I had to be super stoked about mixing detergent to make stretchy slime.

I also had to hide my secret a little better, so I put the stuff behind the actual washing machine. So, every evening it happened, I'd crawl up on my belly and try and yank out the box from behind the machine. Those were some sad and confusing times. The worst part is, if anyone caught wind of Max wetting himself, at almost thirteen, that would kill my rep.

Still, my bygones come nowhere close to your near-death experience. I know life can be pretty shitty sometimes, and yes it not fair that bad things always appear to happen to only good people. It is inevitable that a bad omen is to fall upon genuine folks, and they have done nothing to deserve it. Again, sorry about your mom and your legs.

YEAH, I get you, sorry if I made you uncomfortable. I think I may have hit on you... I only noticed it when I recall the note I sent. I feel better for having told you. It's satisfying you know; I feel good for having done it. So in the future, I won't have to feel like I am dying trying to hold it in.

If you ever need a wingman, even though I am probably crap with girls... well and boys, I'd still like to have the role all the same if you need someone to help you out to steal a girl's heart. Thanks for not getting mad or anything, when I said I liked you. Thanks for everything.

Now I'm not asking you out on a date here if that's what you think I am going to do. However, I'd like you to come and watch me play, rather than just showing up. After the game, we can grab some food and hang for a little bit. The play starts at 7PM on Friday, which is the normal time.

LAST BUT NOT LEAST, it is cool about wanting to click the refresh button and starting all over with our friendship. I have been more honest with you, and you know more things about me than my other best friend who I went to Pre-K with.

THEREFORE, hey, I'm Max Wilson, I'm 14-years-old, I'm in 9th Grade, and not only am I gay, but I am a major thrillseeker, who happens to play piano, sings like a skinned cat, and I served a stretch up in bedwetting state for two years, starting when I was eleven.

GOOD, I'll see you on Friday then, I won't leave you hanging again, I promise.

LATER,
    Max

ENTRY #28

To Max,

IF THIS END'S up being our last letter; I just want you to know, Max, you are a pretty awesome guy. I gratefully appreciate what you did at the game more than you will ever understand. In a way, tonight has restored my spirit in humanity a little more, and the students in this school. I never saw what you were doing, you completely surprised me in the best way imaginable. You know, even if you didn't talk to me the last couple of days, I now realize why. You just needed to adjust to the idea of me being in a wheelchair, and today you proved that you didn't care if we have these subtle differences. Plus, I grasp what you were trying to announce. I realize that you just got a little overwhelmed by all the information, and you perhaps did not know what to do with the knowledge you had been given.

I know you are not that type of guy. I remember sometime in the past you mentioned that you do what feels right, even if it makes you look dumb or appear like a dick. I admire that occupation. Not many people are open to those thoughts. I have heard many times from folks who are afraid to offend other people; even when they need advice or help. I reckon ego gets in the way for many people. I presume that is why pride is one of the seven deadly sins. Capitalizing on your abilities is a favorable notion, just I often find some folks lose themselves when they overindulge. Sure, you must accept and love yourself first before you can learn to help anyone else. Though there is a selfish pride and a gained pride. For at the game, you have gained every ounce of self-assurance you can muster, and I relent in saying that what you have done has made a lonely person feel, simply put, found. I can make out what you must be thinking. How can someone who is seen daily be lost? The excuse is not an example, and neither is the ignorance when self-absorbed minds do not see much further than the current moment and what beverage they will ingest for lunch.

WHEN I TURNED up for the game, I just came, you know, out of respect. You also played pretty well, might I add. At first, I had some trouble trying to find out where you were among the crowd, though I asked a girl sitting next to me did she know what number you are. She gave me the number 11. Nobody picks a number without good cause, and I follow why you choose to have those numerals embodied on your football jersey. If I didn't think otherwise, some girls only turn up to watch you play, and I reached this conclusion when I overheard the same girl sitting to my right, how she thought, and her quote, "that you are sooooo cute."

I can imagine the shock on her face when you go BAM... I'm gay. Then she'll get all crabby, as inherently, I found on a thread online that most girls complain that, as they suggested. "All the gay ones are the good-looking ones."

I'm not sure, if this is true, though I will admit you are sort of intimidating to us guys who are after girls.

THEREFORE, after the fumble incident, I can't believe you made that signal to your coach, and he asked for a timeout. I'll admit, everyone was wondering for a second why he called for a pause in the middle of the game when everything was going okay, even though you were 6 points behind. At first, I didn't think much further than the game, and I did not foresee anything as cool as what was about to happen, and boy was I wrong. I'd have never guessed it could be so wow... it was amazeballs.

After a couple of seconds, your team gathered around and spoke for a moment. The coach met the opposing team captain on the sidelines by the referee. Suddenly everyone dispersed, and well you... You stayed on the sideline and waited until someone handed you a microphone.

Then, Max, you marched out into the middle of the field, removed your helmet, taking a second to brush your hair out of your eyes. Looking around apprehensively, before saying, "Hey everyone, I hope you are enjoying the game. Em... The reason why we've called for a timeout is that I have a very special friend in the audience tonight, and we've planned a little something for him. Em... if Isaac Miller could make his way over here, our team would like him to score our final touchdown for the game."

And like that, I froze. I wasn't sure if I was dreaming or if I had heard you correctly. Except, I couldn't bring myself to move, not an inch. I have always been in the background of people's existence, and then all of a sudden, I have Max

Wilson, the most popular boy in the school asking me to come down to meet him so I can perform a touchdown for our school team.

I glanced around, observing the people surrounding me to see if they had just heard what I was hearing. Apparently, folks didn't know who I was, they just peered on ahead out at you. Where you resorted to shielding your eyes to scan up into the stands as the floodlights towering over you blinded you. When I looked to my dad, who had transported me to the event, as I wasn't allowed out this late in the evening without someone to watch over me.

I heard you called out, "Isaac... The cheeses has gone wild."

Then I smirked and began to giggle. No word of a lie, you looked stupid out there alone after saying that. So, I asked my dad to skedaddle, and I wheeled myself toward you on the field. As I rolled off the concrete, by the edge of the grass, you came to collect me. On the way over you ditched the mic, and one of the players had given you the ball. It was weird, you standing over me. Only you smiled, and that made me feel okay inside. I'm not going to lie, I was terrified, yet at the same time, I was also really excited to be on the field. I guess this was your way of saying, everybody deserves a moment in the spotlight, and you gave it to me.

Precipitation drenched your face in this sheen, and small clumps of hair glued together. I found it amusing how a cow's lick had formed at the back of your head, and I never noticed you had a beauty spot above your lip.

You sheepishly peered at me, and said, "want to score a touchdown together."

I grinned, the sensations that were running through my body then is like nothing I ever felt before. It appeared as if the world was watching us, and I didn't seem to mind that fact since for as long as I can remember, I have always enjoyed avoiding the limelight. Except, a small part of me did want to be acknowledged, just I never imagined it would be like that, on Friday night.

"Cheese gone wild it is," I chuckled.

There was a sparkle in your eye, as your face lit up. You were completely serious. Why so serious?

Then you reached out and placed the football on my lap and said, "hold it tight, okay."

I agreed; you disappeared behind me and took control of my wheelchair, guiding me out into the middle of the field. There was this weird silence from the audience, and also the players on the field. If a pin dropped, you'd be able to distinguish the particular sound. It seemed funny to me at the time that I had the most popular guy in school pushing me along, and nobody cared. So, to break the dreaded silence, I made a joke.

I said, "I'm not sure if my chair is built for speed, but we'll find out when the engine gets going."

Hearing you laugh at my snarkasm, assured me that you do care about me in more ways than I previously thought otherwise. Not long after our laugh, we stood in the center of the field and waited for the time to slip away so that we could make the play and win the game. Resulting in a tie. Although I am not attuned to sports in any fashion, I have to wonder how this worked out. Was it by chance or by complete luck that your team ended up with a tie? I vaguely remember asking you after the game if you planned the draw. Though I think you said no.

When everyone got into place, you rolled me into the middle of the line, where you usually would go, and when the time came to hike, you extracted me from the rush with the ball on my lap. The guy who I had been looking at on the other team, did try to get to me, but not with a rigorous vigor like he'd had torn into you if you had been in my place. I guess you did have a big part in seeing that I got to do this for the first time ever.

And yes, I played some catch with my dad when I was young, and tossed the ball a little. Though I never signed up for football. Sure, my dad watches the Superbowl, just I don't watch it. My mind is preoccupied working on math equations and figuring out the square root of some rock formation. Except, yesterday, when you took off, just the two of us, it felt good with the wind lashing against my face. Even my hair lost direction and disheveled itself with the speed we went. For half a second, I was nervous about the wheelchair tipping, again, I had an excellent navigator. All the players on the field flew by in an instant, and it was over. I scored my first-ever touchdown in American football.

THE SENTIMENT MEANT A LOT, and in the end zone, I looked around noticing people in the stands beginning to clap. I don't think you even had that planned, I recall shifting in my chair and peering over my shoulder to find you quite white in the face, and your ears had gone really red. The game ended on a tie, which is cool. Though thanks for making my life just that little bit better.

I think my dad likes you, well after what you did for me, I guess he does. We walked off the field... well you walked, I wheeled, and my dad came over to meet us. My father asked me when I came home that evening who you were. He wanted to know all the in's and outs regarding our story. I told him that I was assigned a pen pal. I told him about how the two of us first spoke to each other. How we talked about not wanting to refer to one another by a number. Dad has a twisted humor, he found it humorous. Except, it was good seeing him smile for a change, he hasn't been that chirpy since mom died. My dad spends every spare moment he can watching after me, and you know it is annoying, though I know he means well. Plus, yeah, about what happened with my dad on Saturday about him not wanting me to leave with you... I'm sorry about that also. Dads' a worrier now. It probably was incredibly hard for him to have a free night to himself. Back at home, the house stayed quiet for hours. I never imagined how lonely or odd it could be for him until now. Dad has a habit of calling up the hallway to see if I am okay. It's just his thing, only, somewhere in the back of my mind I can picture him still calling out to me in my bedroom, and I'm not there.

Moving on...

Your little brother Jordon is funny... LOL... I like him... he gets my jokes. And it was kind of your mom to invite me over for Jordan's birthday party on Saturday. How she said, "Max and you can do your own thing." I think I'll go to the party.

Coren is cool by the way, I can see why he is your best friend. When we went to the diner, just you and me, I appreciate that you kept it exclusive to us. So, we could talk to each other without me having to meet lots of people all at once.

The restaurant was a nice touch. I'll agree when the two of us waited for the drinks to arrive the silence was incredibly odd. I could tell you were super nervous by the way you kept tugging at your poor ear. When you got talking, however, I must say, you acquire one hell of a stream of consciousness. How is it you do that; skip from subjects and topics? You are a master at communicating it appears, other than when you are super nervous... you turn to a bowl of Jello when confronted with a dilemma.

I don't believe I have ever talked so much, and just being in the same place to have a conversation face to face, it was... Wow. Our meeting went off without a hitch. It had gone a whole deal better than I expected it to go... Not that I was waiting for something to go wrong intentionally.

Just some observations I observed while I was talking to you... I decided you'd like to know. One... you play with your hair way too much. You do this thing that you roll a part of your fringe and keep on twisting it. You also seem to get really excitable at random. I'm also delighted to realize that when you use ketchup, you don't pour it over the food.

The waiter also must know you because she called you by name. It makes me wonder how many times you have been to the eatery.

Next, fries with a milkshake. I'll have to agree it's yum. Thanks for getting me to try it. Dad stopped by the diner yesterday, and I had him get me a milkshake and fries just so I could recreate the taste of the cuisine.

You are remarkably soft and certainly comfortable to talk with. Oh... and you smile like a lot. I saw from the expression in your eyes that it meant a great deal to have me eating with you. I know jitters when I see them. Therefore, to be respectful, even though I didn't interrupt it this way... anybody you will take out on a proper date in the future will be safe in your hands. Hence, thanks for our straight/gay get together. I really enjoyed the company, and I'd love to hang out with you some more.

You know, some girl spoke to me in school today, she said she saw me on the football field and said that it was cool to see me. I don't know what that is supposed to insinuate. Just, I'll agree with what the girl said afterward when she said that it was sweet of you to do that for me.

Friday night was the best nights of my life since the accident... Actually, it was the best night of my life. I'll remember that day for a long time... Perhaps even until I am old and grey. Words do not describe how pleased and appreciative of the time and efforts you have spent talking to me, and also the outside hours working on the surprise.

.

Anyhow, I need to go, I have things to get done before I leave school today. I hope you are having a nice day.

Lastly, if you want to call or message outside of school, my phone number is 202-555-0123 or my Snapchat i.d. is @apunyrocketman

ANYWAY, later,
    Isaac

ENTRY #29

To: @apunyrocketman
From: Max Wilson
10:30PM

HEY ISAAC, I decided to add you on Snapchat. I just want to let you know that Friday was really great. I was delighted that you enjoyed the surprise. I'm still writing my letter to you, though it will be one of my last since we have each other's phone number and Snapchat so we can talk here whenever we feel like it. Not to mention the finish date.

WHEN I WALKED into my English class today, our teacher kindly reminded the classroom, the assignment is due on Friday, and that I needed to write a two-page essay of what I have learned about my other counterpart. I am sad to see that the time is cutting short, just a little. The best part is that I have your phone number and I know who you are so I can pester you any time inside school or out.

. . .

WHAT DO you think about being introduced to my best friend, all the way from Pre-K...? I mean, Coren. I reckon he'd be super excited to meet you and it makes sense if I want to have you around. I mean, I'd like if you'd consider hanging out with me. Coren is pretty much everywhere I hang out. So, I thought I'd try and break the ice so I can invite both of you guys out at the same time in the future. I was thinking tomorrow during lunch, I can meet you at the door to the cafeteria, and I'll bring you over to my table and introduce you to my friends, that is if you don't already have seating arrangements with other peeps.

ANYWAY, I just thought I'd message you, so you had my number, plus, Snapchat info. I hope you are having a nice Monday. So yeah, the phone number is 202-555-5555.

1 NEW MESSAGE
　From: Isaac
　10:51PM

I GOT YOUR MESSAGE, thanks for adding me. I just saved your number. Yeah, I figured we would be stopping any day now, given the closing date is on Friday. We have had ourselves a time, haven't we? Perhaps next year I'll sign up for this program again if it continues to run. It's the best idea I've ever had, and now I have a real friend. This almost feels cliché or something. You know, the type of ending you'd see in a movie, or in Deadpool where Ryan Reynolds turns around and acknowledges the viewers. I can picture it, the superhero pivoting over his shoulder and asking a ridiculous question. Imagine that, that someone was reading our conversations. They'd probably think we'd make a cute couple, though that fact has sailed. Wouldn't that be odd? A part of me, however, wonders what they'd think reading our talks.

I JUST HAD A THOUGHT, but the number of letters we wrote must surely be the length of a book. Well, at least I am assuming now since the notion has come about. Again, I don't think I'd hide anything particular about myself now. I have a great friend like you to lean on when times get tough. Therefore, it makes the blight of bad situations appear non-existent, realizing that someone I trust is going through the same obstacles as me to some degree.

SECONDLY, I don't have to do an essay, as I did the writing buddy thing purely for social interaction. All the same, I believe I will give it a go, even if it's not a full essay, I'm just going to thank the random ideology of luck for his/her wisdom in guiding our two paths closer together so that we could meet.

LASTLY, with lunch, my first initial reaction was to say no, but for the first time ever, I hear myself saying yes. A torrent of questions is flooding my mind, and for the life of me, all I can say is yes. I'm not sure what is happening, but I just want to hang out with you. Before Friday, Max, I was nobody. When I woke on Saturday morning, I had so many people messaging me with warm regards to the touchdown at the game. Messages were coming in from everywhere.

Some people said, "hey I thought what happened at the game was cool," or "sorry I don't talk to you much... I should definitely do it more."

Someone even went on to say this; "your cute, we should talk."

Get this... the person gave me her number. Now you can probably guess that I thought it was a joke. I'm still not sure, I haven't replied to the DMs on Facebook and my other social media stuff, but people notice me more because of what you did, and I don't know how to show my appreciation for what you did. I mean, it just blows all the thank you's out of the water by a long shot, and I don't believe I can ever contend to your gift. That's what it is, a gift, and I thank you for not giving up on our friendship when things got momentarily complicated. I had people I never even knew existed come up to me and talk to me this morning, and it all derived from what you did for me. Therefore, the least I can do is join you for lunch tomorrow and see how it goes from there.

1 New Message
    From: Max
    10:56PM

OMG...OMG... YAY.... Thx u for accepting. I promise you won't regret it. I'm looking forward to tomorrow. You don't need to be nervous or feel like you don't belong among my group of friends. If you are uncomfortable at any time, will you let me know, and I'll try to access the problem? Not that there will be one, everyone was totally cool with you on Friday, so I don't see why things should be different. However, I just want to put it out there in case things are not working for you, or the vibe is not right.

And about the thank you, I don't really know what to say about that. I guess I don't actively go pursing acknowledgment for doing a good deed. I just did what I did... no need for thanks. Just let me hang out with you every so often, and then we will be square.

LOL... you know, I never thought about that before, though, yes, we have written to each other a lot. It's even funnier how since we are phasing out our letters, it does seem like the end of something. Not sure what we are ending, except, it does feel a little odd. I'm not sure what I'd do if I knew other people were reading our conversations. I'm not sure, I'm sort of okay and a little of not. I'm confused. I reckon there are some parts about my life I'd rather wait to figure out and not have exposed if some were to read our letters. The only one who knows about my secret is you, and I'm not ready to come out. I wouldn't want anybody reading what I have written until I am in a better place to handle fallout if there is going to be any. Though you have been completely awesome about the whole situation, so maybe you can help me when I am ready... to come out I mean, but not now. You know the further I dig into this message, I am beginning to wonder why it is necessary in the first place. Why is the default straight? I get it... I know before anybody answers. Though it can be intimidating knowing that what you are supposed to fit in, is not the default. Except, even if it is different for me, I don't believe I hate myself anymore for being this way.

I PRESUME the closest emotion to the feeling I am trying to depict is that I guess I am screwed this way... So, I might as well get on with things. Otherwise, I'll always be depressed and miserable. You know, accept what I can't change. Then in some weird mumbo-jumbo, I'll end up like one of those fairies dancing until 3AM in some gay bar, with a fluffy pink tippet... Yeah, I am shocked too... I had no idea I knew the name of that scarf, but hmm... I have no choice, the condition has always been there, so I reckon what is the worst that can happen by learning to accept it. Hooray for being gay... that's what we say... let's go, not stay.

∼

1 New Message
    From: Isaac
    11:02PM

. . .

HEY, we all have things we like, for me, it's nerdy crap. No word of a lie, but in my bedroom, I have an entire glass cabinet with game memorabilia. Cliché with a cause. If I didn't have a comic book collection or an old-fashioned game console, and I do, might I add. Then I wouldn't be a real geek. Still, I'll never understand how you manage to turn a serious moment into something laughable when you write back to me. You have this funny disposition. Sometimes it seems you try to take life as a pinch of salt; by tossing it over your shoulder and not caring. I'd imagine if I did that the whole shaker would fly out of my hand and knock some poor ninety-year-old out for good. My point in being is, just be you. Dignity and character are much more than a presumption, so don't let the person who makes you... die. You may never know until you have made a transition, but when you open yourself to positive change, when you open your sails wide, to let the wind carry you. It only then feels like life is a breath of fresh air, or how you'll drift in a lucid, semi-conscious state upward. From there, life can only get better.

I'M LOOKING FORWARD to tomorrow too; thanks for not bailing on me now that the end is in sight. It really means a lot to me that you are trying to continue our camaraderie. I'd like nothing more than to contribute to this friendship. Perhaps in a couple of years when we are a little older, mature, wiser even, but completely wild and naïve. I'll still look back at this moment; the two months we shared, and how better my life has gotten since you walked into my exitance. You're okay in my book, I hope I am in yours.

. . .

I'M SURE, everything will go off without a hitch tomorrow, it is the anticipation for what is to come that I am excited of. Plus, I'm just passing on a message as my dad is heading off to bed. So that means I'll be going to sleep in a few minutes too. He just wanted me to tell you that he appreciated what you have done for me. I told him a little bit more about our conversions, and my dad wants me to invite you to dinner on Friday as a thank you. I'd like it if you came... at least let me say thank you. :) Don't leave me hanging with his cooking. LOL... I'm joking he's a good cook.

∽

1 NEW MESSAGE
    From: Max
    11:10PM

LOL... I'll be there... You didn't tell him, did you?

∽

1 NEW MESSAGE
    From: Isaac
    11:11PM

SWEET... Nah... that's on you. Anyway, night, Watson. I'll see you tomorrow.

∽

1 NEW MESSAGE

From: Max
11:11PM

Yep... big day... I'll see you at the cafeteria doors for lunch. Righty-right... Night Sherlock...

Until tomorrow,

Watson. :)

ALSO BY D.K. DANIELS

School is out for the summer and while Max & Issac are now good friends, they are both navigating two entirely different paths. Max is conflicted about his sexual orientation, his relationship with his father and the commitment he feels toward Issac. Except, Max is not the only one suffering. Issac wishes his dad would give him the freedom he'd incredibly desires, the chance to show his new friends just how independent he can be, as his growing popularity becomes a problem.

YOU & I - Book 2

D.K. Daniels

Coming Spring 2020

AFTERWORD

Thank You

If you enjoyed the story, please don't be afraid to reach out to me and let me know what you thought of the book. If you have questions or things you'd like to point out to improve the finished piece, please contact me through my website.

If you appreciated the story let others know you what you read recently :) If it is not too much hassle to leave a review here on Amazon, that would be great... and if you drop one on Goodreads also... I'll love you forever. Reviews help my content reach more people and comfort folks when purchasing some of my work to enjoy.

There is always a new story born each week for me; so, if you enjoyed this: check out my other stories

MyWebsite: dk-daniels.com

I have written over 20 titles available on Patreon, Amazon

and Google Books. Perhaps, you'd be able to find something to indulge for an afternoon or two. If you'd like to stay informed sign up to my mailing list by clicking here. (I never spam and you can unsubscribe whenever you want.)

ABOUT THE AUTHOR

D.K. Daniels writes contemporary/realistic fiction with both teen and college-aged characters aimed at an LGBT audience. His novels often stem from an isolated high-school career and rational outlook on life. For the most part, the stories he writes are about young people finding their way in a noisy world.

D.K. is a major film enthusiast and gamer. His love for storytelling derived from consuming the hours and hours of entertainment during the most isolated years of his teenagehood. Currently living in Ireland, D.K.'s hobby is backed by his amazing boyfriend and loving family.

Follow me on

Printed in Poland
by Amazon Fulfillment
Poland Sp. z o.o., Wrocław